39 DAYS OF
GAZZA

D1637843

39 DAYS OF GAZZA

STEVE PITTS

Pennant Books

First published in paperback 2009
by Pennant Books

Text copyright © 2009 by Steve Pitts

The moral right of the author has been asserted.

All rights reserved. No part of this publication may be reproduced, stored in a retrieval system, or transmitted, in any form or by any means, electronic, mechanical, photocopying, recording or otherwise, without the prior permission in writing of the publisher, except by a reviewer who wishes to quote brief passages in connection with a review written for insertion in a newspaper, magazine or broadcast.

British Library Cataloguing-in-Publication Data:
A catalogue record for this book is available on request from
The British Library

ISBN 978-1-906015-44-2

Designed and typeset by www.envydesign.co.uk

Printed in the UK by CPI William Clowes, Beccles, NR34 7TL

Pictures reproduced with kind permission of Mike Capps/Kappasport, Pete Norton, Action Images and PA Photos.

Every reasonable effort has been made to acknowledge the ownership of copyright material included in this book. Any errors that have inadvertently occurred will be corrected in subsequent editions provided notification is sent to the publisher.

Pennant Books
PO Box 5675
London W1A 3FB

www.pennantbooks.com

CONTENTS

ACKNOWLEDGEMENTS

AS I NOW know, writing a book is very much a team effort and I'd like to thank Jon Dunham, Derek Waugh, Jefferson Lake, Mike Capps and Pete Norton for their much-appreciated professional help. I'd also like to say a big thank you to all the people who gave me their time. I met many great characters along the way and thoroughly enjoyed my hours in the company of a fantastic group of players. Both Ryan-Zico Black and Peter Mallinger have written books about their experiences in football which are well worth a read. *Zico: An Autobiography of a Non-League Footballer* (Black) and *So You Think You Want To Be a Director of a Football Club* (Mallinger) are both published by Authorhouse.

My wife, Leona, never waivered in her support and I love her very much. As I do my wonderful parents, my brothers Mark and Chris, and Lucy, Amy, Jamie, Luky and Nela. And never a day goes by when I don't think of Jan and the boy he would have been. Finally, thanks to Cass

Pennant, for giving me my chance, and to Paul Woods, my editor. Just when I thought I had finished, he pointed out all the flaws and I started all over again. It was exactly what was needed.

1

GAZZA? YOU'RE HAVING A LAUGH!

SHORTLY before midday on 24 September 2005, on a typical Saturday at The Beeswing public house in Kettering, Jim Wykes, the landlord, did what he always does at that time. He left his staff to welcome the lunchtime crowd and climbed the stairs to his private quarters to make himself a bacon buttie and put his feet up. It was 'landlord's hour', and he was only to be disturbed if his sister had nipped over from Melbourne to ask for him. As he hadn't seen her for 40 years, he didn't think that too likely.

Wykes hadn't even got the bacon into the frying pan when he got a call from his barman, Ryan Wilson, summoning him back down to the bar of his recently refurbished pub. 'Has my long-lost sister turned up?' he demanded.

'Better than that,' came the reply. 'It's Paul Gascoigne and Jimmy Five Bellies.'

Wykes, a keen football fan, told Wilson to stop winding him up. Gascoigne was the greatest English footballer of his generation, a huge celebrity who was always in the newspapers for one reason or another. Why would the hero of Italia '90 and Euro '96 be in his pub, a stone's throw from the Rockingham Road home of the non-League football club Kettering Town? But Wilson was adamant it was Gazza.

'I said, "Leave me alone, my bacon's on,"' Wykes recalls. 'I told him they would be lookalikes, that there'd be some sort of competition on in Kettering that afternoon.'

'I'm telling you, Gazza and Five Bellies are sat in your bar watching telly,' Wilson insisted.

Curiosity got the better of the landlord, who went downstairs to see whether he was having his leg pulled. Wykes could only see the back of the two men's heads as they sat facing the large TV screen in the corner. Still sceptical, he stepped out from behind his bar and walked around to stand in front of the pair. All doubts were instantly washed away.

A big man, Wykes knelt down on one knee in front of Gascoigne, who was sitting in a comfy lounge chair. Before he could speak, Gascoigne said to him in his thick Geordie accent, 'You're not proposing to me, are you?'

Wykes laughed, stood up and asked Gascoigne what he was doing in his pub.

'It's all a bit hush-hush, but you'll find out soon enough,' was the reply.

The doors had only just opened and there was only one other person in the bar. 'Leave the lad alone,' Wykes was told.

'But this is *Gazza*,' he replied. 'He's a legend.'

While they spoke, his barman began texting friends to tell them of the celebrity in their midst. They dashed to the pub, saw Gascoigne for themselves and began texting their mates. In a rural market town the size of Kettering news travels quickly, and within 20 minutes the pub was packed with people eager to catch a glimpse of Gascoigne, many clutching their copies of his autobiography, England replica shirts and football programmes for him to sign. Failing that, they grabbed beer mats or simply held out their arm for Gazza to scribble on.

'My daughter's boyfriend told me he was in The Beeswing,' remembers Chris Smith-Haynes, a Conservative councillor for the Kettering Borough Council ward which included Rockingham Road. 'I thought he was talking rubbish.'

On arrival, Gascoigne's close friend, Jimmy 'Five Bellies' Gardner, had ordered a soft drink for himself and a pint of cider for Gascoigne, and, before the pub became swamped, he asked for another cider and a large glass of white wine. 'On the house,' said Wykes, who had to pinch himself to be sure that he was buying a drink for a footballer he had idolised at his peak a decade earlier.

The Beeswing is a large pub, and the rapidly growing crowd began to visibly concern Gascoigne. His mood, chilled on arrival, appeared to darken. 'He was quite happy to sign the autographs at first but when it got too busy he got a bit agitated,' says Wykes. 'He saw all these people piling in and thought any minute the press was going to arrive. Jimmy Five Bellies was asking people to give him some space. He didn't look comfortable.'

Wykes had welcomed the odd celebrity to his pub before, and photos of ex-royal butler and *I'm A Celebrity...* star Paul Burrell as well as former *EastEnders* actor Gary Beadle were on display behind his bar. He asked Gascoigne if he would make it a hat-trick. 'I said to him, "Before you go, my wife would like a picture of you behind the bar with her." He sneered at me, he didn't like that at all. He didn't say anything but just gave me a look that said "no". The way he looked at me, I knew not to push it. He didn't want to be pictured behind a bar.'

It was hardly surprising. With his time as the talisman of English football becoming no more than a memory, Gascoigne had been fighting a long-running and frequently unsuccessful battle against alcoholism and hated the press for the way they had regularly caught him out. Pictures and stories of Gascoigne's drunken escapades were good sellers for the tabloids, and there was no shortage of paparazzi looking to make a few quid for a shot of Gazza with a drink in his hand or staggering out of a nightclub. Gascoigne knew only too well that a photo of him behind a bar, however innocent, could end up embarrassing him in a red-top.

Sadly, Gascoigne had fallen off the wagon so many times since first checking into a drying-out clinic seven years earlier that a picture of him drinking was no longer a surprise. But he had been worshipped by a generation of England football fans and, in a celebrity-obsessed age, he could still shift newspapers. Unfortunately, in the years leading up to his arrival in Kettering, it was nearly always for the wrong reasons: drink, drugs, wife-beating, divorce and a whole host of addictions and personality disorders. When he did make the papers for footballing matters, it was normally only because things had gone wrong yet again.

Everybody queuing for their moment with Gascoigne asked him what he was doing in Kettering. He remained polite but evasive.

Just over an hour after walking into the pub, Gardner shepherded Gascoigne back to his car. As they drove away, a pub full of people pressed their noses to the windows or stepped out into the car park to watch them leave.

The pair didn't have far to go. Kettering Town Football Club is only about 300 yards from The Beeswing, and, as Gardner pulled into the car park that the club shares with the neighbouring bowling alley, the 16-lane Rock 'N' Bowl, it became obvious why Gascoigne was in town. Kettering, known to their fans as the Poppies, were playing an FA Cup second-qualifying-round match against Stafford Rangers that afternoon, and Gazza was there to watch.

Jon Dunham, the football writer who covered the club for the local paper, had arrived at the ground 90 minutes ahead of kick-off, as was his routine, to be breathlessly told of the celebrity drinking a few hundred yards away. By the time he'd convinced himself it wasn't a wind-up and dumped his belongings in the press box to make his way back down the stand, Gascoigne was safely ensconced in the club's boardroom.

Dunham made his way to the social club next to the boardroom, where Gascoigne was the sole topic of conversation among those drinking there, many of whom had wandered along from The Beeswing.

'What's he doing here?' Dunham was asked. 'Is he going to be our new manager?'

At that stage, Dunham didn't know any more than the next guy but resolved to find out, although, with a game to cover, he had to wait until the cup tie had finished before he could approach the man himself.

The match took second place to all the fuss that surrounded Gascoigne's appearance. Prior to kick-off, he had walked up the steps of the main stand to take his seat in the sponsors' section of the well-worn ground with the eyes of the near-1,000-strong crowd firmly fixed on his back.

By that stage, he had been joined by a sizeable entourage including, among others, Gardner, Gascoigne's dad John, former Arsenal midfielder Paul Davis and Andy Billingham, whom Gascoigne had met through promotional work with adidas. Off-the-pitch events with Gazza and his cohorts were proving far more watchable than the hard-fought game, which Kettering won 1–0 thanks to a goal from experienced striker Christian Moore.

After the teams had trooped off at the final whistle, Dunham jogged down from the small press box at the top of the stand to wait near the tunnel entrance while Gascoigne exchanged a few pleasantries with Derek Brown, the team's centre-half and club captain. 'I stood there thinking, "Why on earth would Paul Gascoigne want to be chatting to non-League footballers,"' says Dunham. 'I was thinking to myself, "What's this all about?"'

The rumour that had swept the ground during the game was that Gascoigne was going to be the club's new manager. It sounded no less ridiculous each time it was whispered on, but, eventually, Dunham got his chance to ask Gascoigne if there was any truth in it. Gazza smiled at him, shook his hand, signed an autograph and said, 'No comment.'

Dunham made his way back to the social club believing this was much more than a social visit by the footballing legend, even though the club's chairman, Peter Mallinger, did his best to pass it off as just that when quizzed.

It was chaotic after the game as hundreds of fans scrambled to get close to Gascoigne. People aged from six to sixty, male and female, hard-core fans and celebrity spotters alike, were eager to talk to him, touch him, get him to autograph their programmes or capture the moment on cameraphones.

Dunham spent a couple of hours digging around to try to find out what Gascoigne was doing there. But he didn't get anywhere; amid all the speculation and gossip, anyone with any real information on what Gascoigne was doing at the club was not prepared to talk openly. But he did uncover another story: it seemed that not only was Gascoigne interested in becoming the new manager, but he was also looking to buy the club.

Dunham trusted his source but still found it hard to believe that Kettering Town could be of interest to somebody of Gascoigne's stature in the game. Here was an England legend, capped 57 times for his country, who had played for some of

Europe's top clubs. Kettering Town were so low down the pecking order that they had spent the previous few years in the shadows of Rushden & Diamonds, their despised neighbours a few miles down the road, a club that had been created little more than a decade earlier by Dr Martens mogul Max Griggs.

But a no-comment wasn't a denial – as any journalist knows, it would have taken just one word to kill the rumour stone dead. So, while Gascoigne returned to the boardroom, Dunham telephoned me, his sports editor, with news of the pandemonium at Rockingham Road.

I put the phone down and smiled. As did the editor, Mark Edwards, when he got his call. Mark and I were big football fans with vivid memories of the excitement Gascoigne had whipped up at World Cups and European Championships. And now Gazza was coming to Kettering? Surely, somebody was having a laugh. But what a cracking story, even if only a rumour. If true, it would be the biggest thing to have happened to the club, which, in its 133 years of unassuming existence, had yet to play in the Football League.

It would also be the biggest story of the young sports writer's life, and, if nobody, least of all Gascoigne himself, was going to deny that he was on his way to Kettering Town, then this was a story screaming out for 120-point headlines. Front and back pages.

The following morning, I discussed with Dunham and sub-editor Jim Lyon how to handle the story for the sports supplement that the *Evening Telegraph*, one of two regional daily newspapers in Northamptonshire, published each Monday.

Hard facts were still scarce. So as journalists we did what all hacks do when time is short and a good story is in the offing – we telephoned as many people as we could. Few knew anything, even if they struggled to admit it. Those who claimed an insider's knowledge said they couldn't possibly give up their secrets, but a couple of well-placed people gave off-the-record briefings that all but confirmed it. Paul Gascoigne, England football genius, was in talks about coming to Kettering Town – although whether it was to be as owner, manager, player-manager or director of football was still unclear.

The story was splashed on the front and back pages. Mike Capps, the club photographer who also supplied the paper with pictures, had been stunned to bump into Gascoigne in the car park. He, too, had been clueless as to why Gascoigne was there but that hadn't stopped him shooting as many pictures of the superstar as he could. His long lens focused more on the stand than the game, and the pictures were put to good use accompanying the story on the front page, the back page and spreads comprising just about everything that the internet could churn out about Gascoigne in a few hours on a busy Sunday afternoon. It wasn't all that relevant, but this was Paul Gascoigne. Readers were informed – as if they didn't know already – that Gascoigne had been forced to apologise to the people of Norway after he had told them to 'fuck off', when asked if he had a message for the country ahead of a 1994 World Cup qualifying match. He was only joking, but there were plenty who didn't share his sense of humour.

They were also reminded that Gascoigne had been forced to say sorry to Glasgow Celtic fans after a provocative flute-playing goal celebration, which he repeated a short time later; that he'd been so angry with then England manager Glenn Hoddle that he smashed up a hotel room; that he'd been in and out of rehabilitation clinics; that he'd gone through an unpleasant divorce after a violently abusive marriage; that he was out getting drunk while his wife was giving birth to his baby son, hundreds of miles away.

There was seemingly no end to it.

And still it seemed so unreal. Why Kettering Town? A club in danger of losing its ground in the very near future. A club meandering along some 130 places lower than his hometown club, Newcastle United. A club of insurance salesmen, postmen and warehouse workers who earned a few bob for playing football on Saturdays, and most Tuesdays as well if they could get the time off work. What was it that had caught Gascoigne's eye?

2

FIT TO BE A
MANAGER?

GASCOIGNE'S involvement with Kettering can be traced back to the football ambitions of one man, Imraan Ladak, who had sat anonymously alongside him at the game on that frenetic Saturday in September.

Ladak did nothing to draw attention to himself, as the eyes of the fans were fixed on the man whose dyed blond hair made him easy to pick out from all sides of the ground.

Ladak, originally from Kenya and now living in Milton Keynes, was the chief executive officer of a company supplying locum doctors to the NHS. Still only in his late twenties, he had taken advantage of government deregulation to build up his business to the extent that there was some spare cash burning a hole in his pocket. Ahead of the takeover, *The Times* had reported that his company, DRC Locums, had an annual turnover of £23 million, with registered accounts showing net assets of nearly £1.9 million. He had also expanded into dry-cleaning.

Ladak, a softly spoken Muslim, had clearly done well for himself and quite fancied the idea of a public profile. By the spring of 2005, he had decided to make a move into football and, having worshipped Gascoigne during his four years at Tottenham Hotspur in the early 1990s, Ladak approached people who knew him. And it seemed Gascoigne, looking for a fresh direction to a life that had turned increasingly sour, was happy to talk. They met at Ladak's Milton Keynes home that summer and Gascoigne admitted he had been surprised by Ladak's enthusiasm and knowledge of football. After a three-hour chat, they agreed to work together.

*   *   *

With a potential future in football to refocus his attention, Gascoigne set about getting himself in shape for the challenges ahead. A couple of weeks after his first appearance at Rockingham Road, he underwent an operation on his neck, the 29th on his battered body.

Before then, he had suffered a career-defining injury at the 1991 FA Cup final in which he tore his cruciate knee ligaments in a suicidal tackle after just 17 minutes. His recovery was delayed when he sustained fresh damage to the joint in a nightclub scuffle in Tyneside a few months later.

In a frank interview with Ian Ridley in *The Observer* in February 2003, he had confessed that at least four of his injuries were a direct result of drinking. However, according to Gascoigne, this latest operation had not followed an alcohol-fuelled accident; he had been injured in a fall during a practice session for the Christmas ice-skating special of BBC1's *Strictly Come Dancing* in December 2004.

That was the end of that particular chapter in Gascoigne's attempt to maintain a public profile outside a footballing career in terminal decline. And the man himself was well aware that this injury was more serious than any of his broken bones. Many of the fans who had flocked to Gascoigne on his first public appearance in Kettering had asked him if he was going to play for the club. Gascoigne would have loved nothing more but was afraid of the consequences. 'I've had an operation, so for the next few months I've got to take it easy,' he said at his first press conference. 'I'm scared of another operation. It's not nice having your throat opened up and have them mess with your spine.'

He was still only 38 years old and the previous few years had seen him desperately trying to make up for all the time spent out of the game through injury. He had turned up at some of the most unlikely of destinations in search of a game, none of which went well. A short spell at Boston United as player-coach in 2004 ended with his playing just five matches before walking away. He initially claimed he was going away to get his coaching badges, but later complained the Lincolnshire club had used his name as a marketing tool.

That had followed an even briefer spell in China with Gansu Tianma. If Gascoigne, who had signed a nine-month contract, had been relieved to get home after just four games and two goals, the Chinese were just as happy to see the back of a man who had fled, without warning, to a specialist clinic in Arizona for treatment for his drink problem and depression.

Although his father and Jimmy Gardner had originally gone with him to China, they returned home after a week, and Gascoigne found the isolation in an alien culture, in which he was struggling to learn the language, driving him increasingly to drink. He complained about the air quality, the heat and the standard of football, but what was clear was that he was desperately unhappy.

The dash from China to America wasn't the first time Gascoigne had dropped everything to seek treatment for an overwhelming range of disorders. With great candour, he revealed in his autobiography how he suffered from bulimia, obsessive-compulsive disorder and bipolar disorder, among other conditions.

Even after it was finally confirmed that Gascoigne and Ladak had been in talks to buy Kettering, Gazza continued to attract attention elsewhere. On 18 October, his spokesman was forced to deny he was joining Algarve United in Portugal, with whom he had spent the best part of two months that summer. Ladak, so excited by the proposed takeover he found it hard to keep away from the club, insisted the only reason Gascoigne was absent was out of respect for Kevin Wilson. Jane Morgan Management, who represented Gascoigne, flatly denied he had any intention of signing for the Portuguese club. Gascoigne pointed out that, despite plenty of talk, he was never offered 'anything concrete', although Corrado Correggi, the owner of Algarve United, was urging Gascoigne to accept the coaching role he said he had offered him during his brief spell on Portugal's south coast. 'In England, there are too many people using him,' said Correggi.

Gascoigne had been drinking during that summer, not only wine but also spirits, and a drink-related incident at Gatwick airport saw him banned from a BA flight back to the Algarve, bringing him another round of media criticism after he was seen to grapple with two policemen sent to calm him down. As his father and brother returned to Newcastle, Gascoigne set off for the Bedfordshire health farm Champneys, where he often fled when things got too much.

But, even at this haven, he seemed to find it difficult to keep out of the news and he was taken to hospital, although not required to stay overnight, after eating a poisonous berry while out walking in the grounds. 'I don't know why you are writing this story,' a spokeswoman for Gascoigne told the local paper. 'It was something and nothing. He ate a non-edible berry.'

During this period, Gascoigne went back into hospital to

have the follow-up surgery on his neck as a result of his ice-skating fall. Billingham, acting as Gascoigne's press spokesman, issued a statement saying the timing of the operation had been scheduled so that Gascoigne could 'be fully fit and focused on his new role'. He also said it had been a success. Gascoigne was only in hospital for two days before returning to Champneys. He was helped with his recovery by the backroom team at Arsenal.

As his health began to improve, Gascoigne continued to look for ways to recover his finances, sadly always suspicious that people were trying to 'rip off' his name.

Despite his astonishing earning power in his heyday, he had blown much of his fortune. His personal life had been little short of a disaster and, as a divorced alcoholic who seemed incapable of going too long without a drink, it had taken a heavy toll on his pocket. He was also generous to a fault and had funded houses and holidays, cars and jewellery for family and friends.

He had come to hate the press, believing that what had been printed about him over the previous 20 years had been 'horrific' and 'disgusting'. Despite this, by the time he arrived at Kettering he needed the exposure – and the money – offered by the national newspapers to open his mouth, and his heart, on just about every drama that his life had thrown up.

Eight days after his first appearance in Kettering, in an interview with Anna Kessel in the *Observer*, he revealed how he had been told his financial situation was precarious. The interview had been granted to help promote his soon-to-be-released *Gazza's Golden Balls* DVD, due out before Christmas. 'He asks incredulously … whether it really takes three days for a cheque to clear,' Kessel wrote. Gascoigne focused on his 'props', two mobile phones, a packet of cheap cigarettes and a large cup of coffee, while Kessel studied the 'thin and wan' man sitting in front of her.

As well as carrying out promotional work for the DVD, he revealed plans for a new gadget to make cheaper football boots more effective. 'I've got this thing that goes on the end of a football boot,' he revealed in an interview to promote the DVD. 'Instead of people spending a fortune, they can buy a cheaper pair then put this thing on the toe, which helps you curve the ball. It's going to save families a lot of money.' At this time, he also confessed that 'unfortunately these days I don't get up and just get paid every month. I have to work for a living.'

Perhaps the challenge offered by Ladak had come at just the right time.

3

GAZZAMANIA!

ALTHOUGH Ladak's financial fortunes were heading in the opposite direction to that of his newfound partner, his fortune was far from huge in professional footballing terms. He had looked at both Port Vale and Peterborough United, and admitted he had been 'very impressed' by everything he had seen at the latter. He made an offer which Barry Fry – at various times manager, owner, chairman and director of football at Peterborough – turned down. Less than a year later, Darragh MacAnthony, an Irish multi-millionaire with a personal fortune of £200 million, bought his way into Peterborough. He spent around £5 million in his first year buying out Fry and assembling the most expensive squad in that club's history.

That sort of money was beyond Ladak, and he had to set his sights lower. Fry, one of lower-league football's most endearing characters, pointed him in the direction of Rockingham Road, also believing such a move could be just what Gascoigne needed. 'He'll certainly create loads of enthusiasm and put bums on seats,' he said.

Fry was friendly with Peter Mallinger, the chairman of Kettering Town, who, after a dozen years of limited success, wanted out. He had earned the appreciation, if not enduring love, of supporters for rescuing the club after the previous owner, Mark English, had done a runner to leave it on the brink of closure and at the mercy of police investigations and the Inland Revenue. Mallinger, who had made his money with a string of wool shops, didn't have the financial clout for a serious bid for Football League status, but he steadied a ship that had been heading for the rocks and oversaw a few moments that almost made it all worthwhile, the highlight of which had been a trip to Wembley for the final of the FA Trophy.

He had financed the club to the tune of around £100,000 per season, but even that only kept the club treading water. The possibility of a takeover involving Gascoigne held out the promise of some sort of return on his investment. Perhaps it would even make the perennial dream of a place in the Football League a little more than wishful thinking.

Mallinger had been involved in the boardroom at Newcastle United when a charismatic and supremely talented teenage Gascoigne had first come to nationwide attention with his immense footballing ability and cheeky grin. Gascoigne's star may have faded over the ensuing years, but Mallinger was thrilled that he was being put up as the man to take his club forward.

Although the first public sighting of Gascoigne in Kettering was 24 September, the ball had really begun to roll earlier in the month, after a telephone call between Mallinger and Ladak on 6 September. The two men met in the sponsors' lounge a few days later, and within two hours they had agreed a price. Ladak asked if he could bring Gascoigne along to see the set-up for himself, and a few days before that frenzied Saturday-afternoon visit he had been smuggled into the ground, along with Ladak, to meet with Mallinger in his small office overlooking the pitch.

They kept the lights switched off in the hope that nobody would see Gascoigne and spark the inevitable gossip and rumour. But to no avail. An incredulous player, arriving for training after finishing his day job, had spotted what he was sure was the England legend in the car park, and immediately told the manager, Kevin Wilson.

Wilson had won 42 caps for Northern Ireland in a distinguished playing career that had seen him make more than 600 appearances for the likes of Chelsea, Derby County, Ipswich Town and Walsall. After hanging up his boots, he had gone into coaching, then management, and had been in charge at Kettering for the best part of two years. He recalls looking up to Mallinger's office at the side of the main stand and seeing a crowd of people. Although he couldn't pick Gascoigne out with the lights off, it wasn't hard to put two and two together, especially as he had picked up on the football grapevine that Gascoigne and his business partners had previously shown an interest in buying Peterborough.

Unaware they had been rumbled, the meeting continued. With Ladak and Mallinger having previously shaken hands on a price, there wasn't much else to discuss before the lawyers got to work. Mallinger had been diagnosed with leukaemia shortly before the approach from Ladak and his illness gave him another good reason to get out, while Ladak, the driving force and money-man of the consortium, was keen to get the deal done as quickly as possible. While they talked, Gascoigne ventured to the large window looking out onto the pitch to watch Wilson conducting the training outside.

Mallinger is a true gentleman of the non-League game and Kettering's boardroom hospitality was among the best in semi-professional football. Before his guests had arrived, the consummate host had laid out nibbles, bottles of lager and beer and, conscious of Gascoigne's problems, some bottles of Coca-Cola and Lucozade.

As Mallinger walked, with Ladak, between his own office and the general office next door, he was surprised to hear the drinks cabinet being opened behind him. He turned back to find Gascoigne sitting behind his desk uncorking a bottle of Harvey's Bristol Cream that had been gathering dust, a leftover from the Christmas raffle. When it became clear his guest was going to drink the sherry, Mallinger tentatively offered him a paper cup. Gascoigne waved him away and drank straight from the bottle.

The group stayed in the office for another half-hour or so before Mallinger suggested they walk along the back of the main stand to the sponsors' lounge. Mallinger says he was shocked at Gascoigne's appearance, describing him as 'almost anorexic', and the alcohol worked quickly on his thin frame. As they walked down the steps from the offices, Gascoigne stumbled and needed the help of the ever-present Jimmy Gardner to prevent him falling.

'Imraan had told me that Paul wasn't drinking anymore and I wasn't sure what he'd make of it,' says Mallinger. 'There was him in one room telling me Paul wasn't drinking and Paul in the other room drinking my bottle of Harvey's Bristol Cream. As was often the case with Paul, nobody said anything and we carried on as if nothing had happened. But it was quite surreal.'

In the sponsors' lounge, Gascoigne downed a couple of glasses of white wine, while Mallinger took Ladak to the side of the pitch to be introduced to Wilson. Mallinger told Wilson of the proposed sale, but there was no mention of Gascoigne's involvement at this stage, although a few days later Ladak met Wilson and told him of his plan to make Gascoigne manager. Wilson was assured there would be a role for him on the same wages.

Although there had been strong speculation that Gascoigne was buying a share in the club, he did not put his hand in his pocket. Ladak had agreed a price with Mallinger, £160,000 for outright ownership, and the deal was that Gascoigne would put up around 30 per cent of the money needed to buy out Mallinger and minor shareholder Trevor Bennett. He would then not take a salary for his first five months as manager as they implemented their business plan.

As it turned out, despite promises that Gascoigne's share was on its way, Ladak would never see a penny, and there was speculation as mid-October approached that the deal had fallen through. But, following the 3–0 FA Cup fourth-qualifying-round victory over Gravesend & Northfleet on 22 October, an impressive result against a team doing well in the division above, Ladak claimed the deal should be concluded within a few days.

His optimism was the result of further talks with the accommodating Mallinger. With Gascoigne's money not forthcoming, Ladak had sought a revised agreement whereby Mallinger would be paid the same price but with the share supposedly being put up by Gascoigne paid in instalments. 40 months after the handover, Mallinger had still not received all he was due.

Ladak has been asked many times since why he took the gamble on someone as unstable as Gascoigne had proved to be in the years prior to the pair putting their 'consortium' together.

But he had been bewitched by the Gascoigne who scored a spectacular goal for Spurs against bitter rivals Arsenal in the FA Cup semi-final of 1991, on his way to becoming a national icon. Gazza was a Tottenham and England legend. Here was Ladak, a young man with no experience of football other than as a fan, working in partnership with his boyhood hero on an exciting new venture that would surely lead to bigger and better things. And he had put it all together, even if that had required little more than a telephone call and a three-hour conversation – and, of course, a significant amount of money.

'It was a call out of the blue,' Ladak said when asked to explain why he had gone after Gascoigne. 'The three players I've admired most are Maradona, Ronaldinho and Paul. Ronaldinho's under contract and Maradona's not really management material.' But was Gascoigne?

Gascoigne had convinced him that he could keep his drinking, and other problems, under control, and Ladak was having no truck with the doubters. He was keen to assure people that Gascoigne was a reformed character who was as committed to Kettering Town as he was. 'From what I've heard, the one worry that people have got is that Paul may not be around for that long,' he admitted to reporter Jon Dunham. 'He has invested in the club. He is part of the consortium and he will be involved in the long term.'

Although he did not always answer his phone, Gascoigne gave every indication of having a genuine passion for the task ahead. While he was recovering from the operation on his neck, he often retreated to Champneys. There he had been transformed from the thin and wan man who had so disappointed Anna Kessel and shocked Mallinger to someone who appeared in reasonable health, other than having a big plaster on his neck, when he was unveiled as manager three-and-a-half weeks after Kessel's *Observer* article was published. The pictures taken during and after the press conference on 27 October show a man enjoying being back in the limelight for purely footballing reasons. He was the charming, wise-cracking man who had captivated the nation, and it was good to see.

When Ladak spoke to him in the weeks leading up to that press conference, Gascoigne could be humble and keen to impress, even though he had found it odd being interviewed for a job by a man 10 years his junior. He studied videos of Kettering playing, and they talked about the type of players they should recruit. The disgraced former Manchester United and Chelsea player Mark Bosnich was mentioned as a possible goalkeeper. Other names bandied about included former England strikers Les Ferdinand, Teddy Sheringham and Steve McManaman.

Ladak could barely contain himself and spoke of signing 'very big former internationals who have played Champions League football'. When the name of Graeme Le Saux, capped 36 times by England, was speculatively thrown into the hat, Ladak retorted, 'Bigger than that.'

Ladak and Gascoigne also spent time discussing how they would take the playing staff full-time and introduce a reserve team, something that had been beyond the means of Mallinger. The Football League was the target – in three to five years, according to Gascoigne, who had convinced Ladak that he was not at fault for his rapid departure from his three previous ventures, as far apart as Lincolnshire, China and the Algarve. That was in the past and he had got his act together. He would deliver, and Ladak was willing to put his faith in a man he had idolised from the White Hart Lane stands.

Ladak, like so many over the years, was determined to give him the benefit of the doubt. He knew that Gascoigne's name alone would bring in the crowds and he gave every impression that Kettering Town could *blitzkrieg* their way into the Football League. Gascoigne was just the man for attracting the players needed to achieve that goal.

Even those who thought his ambition naive at this ruthless level of semi-professional football lauded his enthusiasm. And Gascoigne had another big advantage: his name alone would open the door to potential sponsors. Gascoigne claimed as many as 40 were keen to get involved with him at Kettering.

The promises that he made to Ladak were the same ones he went on to make to the supporters of the club and the people of Kettering in general. Aware that his first venture into football management after years of negative headlines had attracted scepticism, Gascoigne met the critics head-on: 'I'm not going in there saying, "I'm Paul Gascoigne, I want respect." But I've always been a good person and that's why I've never fallen out with any of the managers I've worked with these past 23 years. They respect me and not one has advised me not to do it. I've just got to make sure I do the right things as a manager. I won't be making the club look like a circus. I shall be doing the job properly like the top managers.'

He wanted to be judged at face value, not by what the good folk of Kettering had been reading in their newspapers: 'Local people will get to know me and when they do they will realise that I am an honest and genuine guy, and I will always try and give a good account of what's happening at the football club.'

And he did try. After the game against Stafford Rangers, he had spent a good half-hour signing autographs, posing for pictures, shaking hands and exchanging small talk with a queue of excited football fans, young and old, which snaked around the back of the stand. He had stepped out from the boardroom to meet them with a smile on his face after a crowd had gathered around the entrance to chorus, 'Gazza, Gazza, Gazza' without a break for 20 minutes. They gave every indication they would carry on all night if necessary, and he clearly enjoyed the adulation. Mike Capps recalls, 'They were asking him to sign just about anything ... shirts, programmes, bits of card. If the kids had picked stones up off the ground, he'd have signed them.'

Indeed, for much of his time at Kettering, Gascoigne demonstrated a tolerance of supporters that put to shame those who would sneak out through side doors to avoid pesky fans. He was a genuine man of the people. Many top footballers, and other sportsmen, refuse to sign autographs for fear of them ending up on eBay or endorsing dodgy products. Gascoigne would sign almost anything put in front of him. He seemed to find it hard to say no.

And so Gazzamania came to Kettering, and it wasn't only football fans who were whipped into a state of great excitement at the prospect of Gascoigne picking their team. The local MP, councillors of all political persuasions, business leaders and the solid, ordinary folk of a town hardly renowned for its football hysteria all threw their arms open to a man they felt was going to put Kettering in the spotlight. 'To say the club had been put on the map nationally and internationally would be an understatement,' says Kevin Meikle, who, in the way only sport seems to manage, got himself promoted from loyal fan to managing director in the aftermath of the takeover.

Local councillor Chris Smith-Haynes says there was 'absolute elation' in her neighbourhood at the news that Gascoigne was to be the club's manager. 'It was like the second coming,' she enthuses. 'There was great excitement. People were stopping and talking in the streets; there was a feel-good factor.'

Kettering MP Philip Hollobone couldn't contain his enthusiasm as he predicted a positive impact 'on all businesses and shops in the town'. The Tory politician gushed, 'It is great for Kettering that a footballer as professional as Paul Gascoigne should take an interest in our main local football club.' Gazza-inspired graffiti began appearing on the walls of buildings and fences in Kettering as the excitement spread. 'Welcome to Kettering Gazza' and 'Gazza's Army' were among the sentiments spray-painted in the town centre.

As for the players, there was genuine excitement at the prospect of playing for a man they all claimed as their favourite footballer, even if there was regret over the obvious shadow cast over Wilson's future. 'When I was a kid, Paul Gascoigne was my hero and the chance to meet Gazza, it's like you're really nervous,' said Wayne Diuk, a defender in his seventh season with the club. 'But a lot of us were loyal to Kev and we were thinking, "If Gazza's coming in, then where's Kev going?" I didn't want to see him stitched up.'

Andy Hall, a teenager busy trying to establish himself in the team, said, 'When it was first being said, I just thought it was all talk. Then Gazza walks into the dressing room and he's standing there, and you think, "Hey, this is an opportunity for me."'

More experienced players found it hard to take it in. Christian Moore, a no-nonsense veteran of the non-League game at the age of 32, said Gascoigne had won a special place in his heart when, as a teenager, he had watched him at the 1990 World Cup finals. Moore's striker partner, Neil Midgley, a lifelong Tottenham supporter, answered his phone to find Paul Davis telling him he had Paul Gascoigne wanting to speak to him. Midgley was so excited he jumped out of his chair to stand almost to attention as he spoke to the legend. 'I felt like I should be saluting,' he recalls. 'Gascoigne was a big, big hero of mine. I kept telling myself, "It's Paul Gascoigne, I'm going to be playing for Gazza. I'm going to do my best to make sure I'm a part of this."'

*   *   *

Although the majority of fans were thrilled at the prospect of Gascoigne coming to Kettering, club director Dave Dunham remained one of a sizeable minority who had to be convinced. 'It had been put through Imraan that Gascoigne's problems had been well documented but that he was reformed and recovered and was able to take the job on,' he recalled. 'But it was fairly obvious to me from the outset that he hadn't and he wasn't able to do it. Everyone was aware of Gascoigne's history. Unless he was a completely reformed character, I just wondered how it was going to be possible.'

However much those behind Gascoigne hoped he had his alcoholism under control, he had been seen drinking wine, cider, brandy and sherry at the club and around the town even before he had moved into the manager's office. The newspapers had found out about Gascoigne's session in The Beeswing, and landlord Jim Wykes's phone lines were red hot with calls from journalists asking what he had been drinking and whether he had behaved himself. To protect his idol, Wykes told them he had only had soda water and not the cider and large glass of white wine that Gascoigne had drunk.

Wykes said Gascoigne did not appear affected by the alcohol on leaving the pub. But it seemed he had caused offence in the club's boardroom a short while later by spitting a mouthful of wine out onto the carpet, apparently without a second thought. At a club which prided itself on its hospitality, the reaction was one of silent horror. 'This was Paul Gascoigne and people had stars in their eyes,' said Dave Dunham. 'But what do you do? Nobody said anything and it was just cleared up.'

Mallinger – who, until the time he stood down as chairman, was a stickler for standards and insisted that visitors to his boardroom wore a jacket and tie – was mortified. Not least for his wife, Barbara, who had to mop up the spillage, while Gascoigne stood nearby causing further offence in what was typically a rather genteel environment with language peppered with expletives.

With the deal yet to be completed, Gascoigne went off to conduct more interviews to promote his DVD and look for other ways to make money, always suspicious that some people were trying to exploit him.

Meanwhile, Ladak busied himself with the club he was about to take charge of. He went along to Compton Park, the Northampton home of the United Counties League side Cogenhoe United, to watch what was basically a youth team lose 2–1 in the Northamptonshire Football Association's Hillier Cup.

He was regularly in touch with those at the club and a few alarm bells had already sounded with Wilson over the way that Ladak would seek him out for a chat about the team. He felt uncomfortable discussing selections, substitutions and tactics with somebody he barely knew. And it was an issue that would be central to Gascoigne's list of complaints less than two months later.

Somebody else not at ease was Wilson's second in command, Alan Biley. The striker had enjoyed a lengthy playing career with the likes of Everton, Portsmouth, Derby County and Cambridge United before coaching in America, Holland and Greece. He had then settled into the non-League game and joined his former Derby teammate Wilson as assistant manager in February 2004, shortly after Wilson's appointment.

Biley had seen Ladak watching training and initiating discussions, and approached Wilson to explain his doubts. 'I'm not sure I want to be here,' he confided to the manager.

Wilson left it to Biley to make his own decision, and on the eve of the FA Cup third-qualifying-round trip to St Albans on 8 October he informed Wilson that he was leaving. The game was important to Kettering because victory would leave them one round away from the first round proper and the possibility of a lucrative tie against a League club. As they travelled to Hertfordshire, Wilson told the players that Biley was unwell, only giving them the true story after the goalless draw.

Three days later, Kettering, their results improving by the week, thumped St Albans 4–0 in the replay at Rockingham

Road in front of a Tuesday evening crowd of more than 1,200 fans. The following Saturday's 4–0 league defeat of Leigh RMI saw an almost identical attendance. The Gazza effect was becoming evident. Prior to his first appearance at the club, the Poppies had played four home league games and had averaged 912, with a highest gate of 966. By the time they took on Gravesend & Northfleet on 22 October, the final game before Gascoigne's appointment after a month of relentless speculation, the attendance had climbed to 1,647.

Like many of the fans awaiting the arrival of the living legend, Ladak may well have looked at his boyhood hero through rose-tinted glasses. But he was only one of many people willing Gascoigne to seize this opportunity. Despite the well-documented problems he may have had since his days as England's talisman, there was still plenty of goodwill and affection for him.

One of those prepared to throw his hat into the ring with Gascoigne was Paul Davis, who had been involved in professional football for his entire adult life, having signed as an apprentice for Arsenal at the age of 16. He went on to become a key member of the dominant Gunners side of the late 1980s and early 1990s, picking up medals as a First Division, FA Cup, League Cup and European Cup Winners Cup winner. Although, unlike Gascoigne, this quietly spoken Londoner did not play for the full England team, he was capped at Under-21 level on his way to 447 appearances for Arsenal, scoring 37 goals in his 17 years at Highbury.

After his playing career had ended with a brief spell at Brentford, Davis went into coaching with the football love of his life, Arsenal, and became a qualified FA coach. Like Ladak, Davis was hopeful that Gascoigne could make a success of the Kettering Town job, and agreed to join him as assistant manager. He, too, bought into Gascoigne's vision. 'He is still the passionate, enthusiastic guy he was when I first played against him when he was 17,' Davis stressed. 'He has enormous qualities that he can pass on to younger players.'

Of course, Davis was aware of the problems that had haunted Gascoigne over the previous decade, but thought the new venture could keep him focused on football. 'We only look at the positive side of Paul,' he pointed out.

Davis also hoped that assuming managerial responsibility for a squad of footballers who would obviously look up to him would help bring out the best in Gascoigne. In purely footballing terms, he was a genius who had played under some of the best managers in the business. He could draw on the experience gained from working for the likes of Terry Venables (QPR, Tottenham, Barcelona, England), Walter Smith (Glasgow Rangers, Everton, Scotland) and Bobby Robson (Ipswich, Newcastle, Porto, Barcelona, England). If he could combine that with his outstanding football instincts, while maintaining sobriety and interest, Davis felt he had a chance of taking the first steps on what Gascoigne was hopeful would be a long career in football management. But, as always, matters unrelated to his footballing ability would decide whether that would be possible.

Venables, Smith and Robson were among the many big names to send Gascoigne messages of support. Like so many others, they must have had their fingers crossed. They knew that, if all went well, it could help him to begin to deal with the mental-health issues that had caused him so much suffering.

*   *   *

As the pro-Gazza graffiti began appearing on the walls in the town centre, so one of the questions asked at the time was how many other footballers could have generated such excitement in a town like Kettering? Sure, the club could claim the likes of Tommy Lawton, Derek Dougan and Ron

Atkinson among its former managers, but it had never made it into the League and was hardly a hotbed of football fever.

'You have to ask yourself who else would get the town that excited,' Mallinger wondered. 'I can't think of anybody. He's just one of his own, unique. And if he turned up sober now and did it all again he'd get the same reaction.'

Even Dave Dunham, who had grave doubts about the project from the moment he first met Gascoigne in the boardroom prior to the takeover, admitted he would struggle to name any other Englishman, other than David Beckham, who could have had whipped up such a storm.

'If it had been somebody of Gascoigne's standing in football but without everything else that goes on around him, would there have been the same reaction?' he speculated. 'If it had been any of his teammates from that Euro '96 team, such as Gareth Southgate or Stuart Pearce, would everybody have got so worked up? I don't think so. But it was Gascoigne and he has always had that sort of aura. There were a lot of people in Kettering who were just overtaken by it all.'

Dunham had been deeply unimpressed when meeting Gascoigne for the first time. Gascoigne had finished his session in The Beeswing and arrived in the boardroom shortly before 2pm – two-and-a-half hours later than the agreed itinerary – and Dunham firmly believed from that moment on that Gascoigne's involvement would end in tears. But, despite his misgivings, even he was moved to admit, 'As for putting the club in the local, national and international domain, it was fantastic. Perhaps that was Imraan Ladak's intention all along.'

However, even Ladak was surprised by the level of interest shown in Gascoigne. Despite agreeing with Mallinger not to comment publicly until the agreement was signed, he was unable to stop himself sharing his thoughts with the local paper. 'The phone hasn't stopped ringing,' he said. 'I knew the fact that Paul was involved would attract media attention but it has gone way beyond what I expected.'

And he wasn't the only one. Mallinger found it impossible to concentrate on everyday business as the few phones at the ground rang incessantly. 'As soon as we confirmed Paul Gascoigne was to be involved, the media were almost permanently camped on our doorstep,' he recalls. 'Sky TV made Rockingham Road their second home and other TV and radio stations from all over the world were constantly on the telephone. I was telephoned by a radio station in Melbourne on my way home in the evening to talk live on their morning programme.' What did he tell them? 'Anything I could think of about Paul. If anything, he was even bigger news over there.'

The fascination with Gascoigne seemed without limit, and the media storm was to become even more intense as the press conference was staged to unveil 'Paul Gascoigne the manager' to the waiting world.

4

I KNOW WHAT THEY'RE SAYING – AND I'LL PROVE THEM WRONG!

PRESS conferences at Rockingham Road were few and far between. Why would a Conference North club go to the bother of organising a media gathering when a good turnout would be two people, Jon Dunham for the local paper and perhaps somebody from BBC Radio Northampton.

Away from the games, the manager typically met Dunham once a week, normally a Thursday lunchtime, to discuss the forthcoming weekend fixture. But if the manager or chairman, or anybody else for that matter, wanted to impart news or request a plug, it was just as easy to pick up the phone.

If the story on 27 October 2005 had been the departure of Mallinger as chairman and the arrival of Ladak, with Wilson staying on as manager, a press conference would have been pointless. However, the story that day wasn't merely the change of personnel at a minor-league club. The press had been invited for the unveiling of one of the worst-kept secrets in football: Paul Gascoigne's first job as a football club manager. And some 70 print journalists, six TV crews and a clutch of radio reporters had squeezed into the social club which had been spruced up for the big event, as there was no other room big enough for such a gathering.

No doubt many of those seasoned journalists making their way to the club would have been cynical both about Gascoigne's motives and his chances of making a success at a football club so far below his previous level. Plenty of them had seen it all before, having passed on Gazza's good intentions to their readers as he embarked on yet another venture, only to have to report on the almost inevitable failure a short while later. Nevertheless, this was a man who had given many of them moments to lift them out of their press-box seats, plus some laughs, during his playing days, and there was definitely a certain amount of sympathy and affection for him.

Jon Dunham arrived at his office a mile from the ground and switched on the sports-desk television to see the Sky Sports News 9am headlines reporting live from outside Rockingham Road. The press conference wasn't scheduled to get under way until 11am, and Sky was doing its best to whip up hysteria in the club's deserted car park. Dunham began to realise quite how big this story was.

But, had he been in any doubt, the journalist from Rome who had flown in to cover the story for followers of the Serie A club Lazio would have convinced him. More than a decade after Gascoigne's stint with their team, they still had great fondness for a footballer who may have played only 39 league matches over two years but who had captivated them with moments of sheer brilliance on the pitch, scored a winning goal against hated rivals Roma and made them laugh – even when he was being fined £9,000 for belching into a television microphone when asked how he felt about being dropped.

The start of the press conference was delayed, so the photographers further jockeyed for position and a few more chairs were squeezed in for the late arrivals. The seating order followed a rough pattern of photographers at the front, print journalists behind them, TV cameramen in an arc behind them and TV reporters and radio men hanging around at the back and to the sides, in the hope of securing one-to-one interviews later. It was clearly going to be a long day.

Pressing their noses against the windows was a group of supporters in their dozens who had come along to witness a historic event in their club's history. With more intimate knowledge of the club than either those who had organised the press conference or those journalists attending it, several sneaked inside to watch from behind the TV cameramen.

Waiting to face the press was Billingham, the self-appointed host for the day, Mallinger, Wilson, Ladak, Gascoigne, Davis and Mick Leech, a Kettering stalwart who was a personal friend of Mallinger. Like the other directors, he was standing down. The new regime was coming in with its own personnel and ideas.

Gascoigne sat down to answer questions from the assembled journalists. He was wearing an open-necked, long-collared shirt that did nothing to hide the prominent white plaster on his neck, which was covering his recent operation scar.

Gascoigne clearly couldn't wait to get going. In his difficult relationship with the press, he may have found much of what had been written about him to be 'disgusting', but he was evidently happy to talk about this new venture. For the first time in a long while, most of the questions were about football and a future in the game. He was positive, upbeat, charming and convincing. There were none of the nervous twitches and afflictions that were to become apparent only a week later.

Gascoigne and Ladak had both prepared statements, and were happy to answer questions before stepping out onto the pitch for more pictures and a series of television, radio and one-to-one newspaper interviews.

Even those who felt Gascoigne was the wrong man at the wrong club seemed to want him to prove them wrong, and they listened attentively as he spoke about a club which had only come to their attention because of his involvement. Davis was to be head coach, Wilson director of football, and Billingham and Ladak the men he was to work with off the pitch to generate the cash for a push into the Football League. 'This club hasn't been in the Football League for 133 years so that's one of our main objectives,' he said. 'It's something for the supporters to look forward to. It's going to be a big thing for us.'

There was no doubt he believed it was possible, just as he believed he had committed himself to a long-term future at the club. And when he was talking about football he was happy to speak for as long as there was someone to listen to him: 'I will be spending plenty of time looking at the current squad, working with my assistant manager Paul Davis and Kevin on the strengths and weaknesses of our players and hopefully looking to add some fresh faces where required. We will be working hard to achieve promotion this season. But if not we will regroup and build on the positives of the team to target automatic promotion next season.'

Gascoigne was taking over a team which – under the leadership of Wilson but with an eye on the imminent arrival of their manager-to-be – had gone five games without conceding a goal and had climbed into the Conference North top five. They had also earned a place in the first round proper of the FA Cup.

Things were going so well on the pitch that Wilson, understandably, felt too much change too soon could only be disruptive: 'I felt it might have been better if I'd stayed as manager and Paul Gascoigne came in as director of football. If they had wanted to bring Paul Davis in they could have done that as coach. That would have kept a bit of continuity.

'I understood if they decided in the longer term Paul was going to become the manager, all well and good. I just felt it was too sudden, a bit too much of a change too quickly, too many new ideas. With players at non-League level, you have to bring ideas in slowly. Everything was being rushed.'

He also had other concerns. While the focus was naturally almost exclusively on Gascoigne, Wilson sat two seats along from the new manager and was practically squirming in his seat. Of all the places he wanted to be on that Thursday morning, an event being shown live on television was probably the last. He had been unable to make up his mind whether he wanted to be part of the new set-up, forced into a different role which diminished his relationship with the players, and was agonising over whether to walk away.

Adding to his unease, he was off sick with tonsillitis from his day job, and knew it was not going to go down well with his employers at a Northampton roofing company when pictures of him in a suit and tie were beamed into homes up and down the country. 'I sat there wishing I wasn't there, feeling like a spare prick at a wedding,' says Wilson. 'Everyone I speak to says, "You didn't look very happy," and I say, "Would you have liked it if it was happening to you?" I was the manager who had been dethroned.'

Wilson had loved working for Mallinger despite the financial pressures, but felt the role Gascoigne had earmarked for him was little more than an attempt to distance him from the players he had managed over the previous 21 months.

'They called it director of football but to me it looked like a glorified chief scout,' says Wilson. 'He [Gascoigne] didn't want me in the dressing room, he didn't want me around the players, he didn't want me at training. That wasn't what I had been told initially. I was told by Mr Ladak that I'd be director of football, that I'd be involved in everything, I'd be hands on. My money was going to be the same, but that wasn't the point. It wasn't the job for me. I don't blame Paul Gascoigne for that, it's one of those situations that happens in football.'

*   *   *

After the formal press conference had concluded, Jon Dunham took a seat alongside Gascoigne in the small home dug-out in front of the main stand and, with the takeover story in the bag and thousands of words from the new Poppies manager in his notebook from the press conference, set about asking questions that only fans of the club, rather than the public at large, needed answers to.

'With all the other stuff covered at the press conference, the first thing I wanted to talk to him about was that weekend's game against Droylsden,' says Dunham. 'They were right up there with Kettering and it was a really big game for them. He seemed to enjoy the opportunity to talk as a football manager and we spoke about Droylsden.'

Did he know what he was talking about?

'To a certain extent he did. He seemed to know a bit about Droylsden.'

Those niche questions had been few and far between when everybody was sitting in the social club a short while earlier. Despite his attempt to look forward, he was still occasionally dragged back to the failures of the past and was keen to point out the differences between his experiences at Boston United, Gansu Tianma and Algarve United and what he was taking on. 'I was used there for publicity,' he explained. 'My name is seen by many as a marketing tool that can create publicity, contacts and ultimately money for their own football club.

'Kettering Town is a different proposition for me as I'm investing my personal money in return for a substantial stake in the club and a seat on the board of directors. So not only will I be manager working hard to win games for the supporters and everybody concerned with the club, but I will also be a director working hard to achieve the club's financial goals. My long-term goal is to become a top-class manager and I'm delighted that I am beginning my journey here at Rockingham Road.'

Jon Dunham had been happy to get his 10 minutes with the new manager, and a few pictures of them together, before Gascoigne was dragged away to be quizzed in an endless round of interviews. He had adored Gascoigne the player, but felt up close the new manager did not look quite as well as he had from just a few feet at the formal press conference.

'Close up he looked frail, he didn't look like someone who was ready to be a manager at any level,' said Dunham. 'He seemed to appreciate talking to me about the players and the next game but he also wanted to be asked about his goal in Euro '96 and Italia '90, and even the darker times with his injuries. He enjoyed the attention completely.'

As Dunham conducted his interview with Gascoigne, the TV crews set up on the pitch and waited for Billingham to grab the star turn and lead him from one microphone to the next. With time on their hands, they interviewed pretty much anybody who would stand still for two minutes.

Ross Patrick was a supporter who had waited outside the social club for two hours before finally talking his way past the stewards on the door. He found himself giving interviews to Sky Sports News, the BBC and ITV and then got to meet Gascoigne, who signed his Poppies shirt: 'Although he was clearly tired, he gave the supporters his time, which was fantastic.'

As the media kerfuffle finally began to die down, Patrick headed back to the bar, where the former Tottenham and Manchester United striker Garth Crooks, who had interviewed Gascoigne for the following Saturday's *Football Focus* programme, was already seated. He bought a round for everybody in the social club and spent 45 minutes chatting to the fans.

Patrick's day became even more surreal when Ladak popped in and invited him and a friend to be his guests for his first match as chairman. They got to meet Gascoigne ahead of the game, who joked they were in the team and told Patrick he 'shouldn't lose a header'.

Peter Short, the matchday programme editor, wrote a column called 'Shorty says' in which he explained how the Gascoigne-inspired media attention was having a huge impact on both club and town. There had been a notable increase in the number of Kettering shirts being spotted on the streets and, wherever he went, the football club had become the main topic of conversation: 'And don't even get me started on taxi drivers who seem to know everything from what Mr Gascoigne had for dinner to the exact number of column inches that KTFC got in *The Times*.'

But he did question how long the interest could be sustained at a level unique for a non-League football club: 'How many more times will I be tuning in to Sky Sports news? How many more times will Mark Pougatch say "Kettering Town" on Radio 5 Live? How many more taxi drivers do I need to have the same conversation with again and again?' Shorty confessed to having no idea. 'But I intend to lap up every second,' he revealed.

Mike Capps had broken off a family holiday in the West Country to return for the press conference. More often than not, when anything happened at Rockingham Road he was the only photographer present. But it wasn't the case today, and he spent a couple of hours doing his best to ensure he captured every single moment of a dramatic day, and was determined to be the last snapper to leave the ground. As the national press finally departed, Capps found himself sitting alone in the main stand with Gascoigne: 'He had posed for hundreds of pictures but I asked him if I could take a few more of him with a Kettering shirt. He was happy to do it.

'I had been introduced to him as the club photographer and I told him that if there was ever anything he didn't want me to take a picture of to just tell me. He said, "You've got your job to do and I've got mine. If there's something I don't want you to take I'll tell you soon enough. I'll shove you out of the way."'

*   *   *

Ladak had revealed in his statement that the deal had not been completely finalised and that 'we expect to have the final paperwork signed before Saturday's game'. To prevent it from collapsing, Mallinger had agreed to the revised payment plan suggested by Ladak following his failure to get any money off Gascoigne. Gascoigne admitted he had agreed to put up £50,000 but said he did not hand over the cash because, despite repeated requests, he couldn't get a contract from Ladak.

Although he was not yet the official owner, nothing was going to stop Ladak outlining his plans for a club which he said represented everything that was good about football: 'Real supporters watching their home-town team because they love football, not glory. Real players in the non-League because they love football, not money. A real stadium with terraces and an atmosphere the players can feel.'

He went on to explain the early priorities were a full-time playing squad, a solution to the stadium issue that had haunted Mallinger as the years on the lease ran down to single figures and building an infrastructure to allow the club to get into the Football League.

And his take on Gascoigne's appointment? 'One of England's finest joining to help fulfil the dreams of supporters and players,' he insisted. According to Ladak, it was the potential of the club, 'with possibly the largest fan-base in non-League football', that had attracted Gascoigne: 'Paul has been determined to wait for the right club before committing his future and the fact that he is part of this consortium illustrates his confidence in the project.'

However, Gascoigne was already having doubts over his relationship with Ladak, and the lack of a formal contract was a frustration. 'I saw one once, but then he took it back,' he later said. He complained of being 'stitched up', although at the time of the press conference the lure of a return to football was enough to buy his silence.

Ladak was in a hurry to stamp his mark on the club, and wanted to get cracking. The previous directors might still have been listed among the club officials in the matchday programme for the cup tie against Stevenage Borough on 5 November, but Ladak had told them they had done their bit and it was now time for them to sit back and enjoy the football.

'My perception was he wanted to run the club his way, which was fine,' said Dave Dunham. 'That was his privilege. From a personal point of view, given that he didn't have any experience of running a football club at all, I probably did wonder if he would benefit from having some help. Imraan was very ambitious and very enthusiastic. I don't know how much knowledge he had about how non-League football works but I think Imraan would probably say himself that it has been a huge learning curve and he might have done things differently if he could have his time again.'

For Ladak and Gascoigne, however, their lack of knowledge at this level was not something that troubled them. They were both confident in their own ability to get stuck into their ambitious plans, and Gascoigne was quick to establish his hierarchy, making clear that Davis would be his right-hand man while he expected Wilson to look at potential new recruits 'when we get the money' and to scout forthcoming opponents. As for himself, he said, 'I'll be picking the team and deciding tactics, who comes off, who comes on as sub.'

*   *   *

Mallinger had watched Gacoigne being chased around the pitch. He had sold the club with a heavy heart and would virtually need to be dragged out of the boardroom. Like Dave Dunham and Wilson, he had been hoping the new regime would not cut all ties with the people who had run the club to that point.

Although Mallinger did stay on to help smooth the transition, he eventually started feeling both left out and squeezed out. Others around the club, who had been appointed by Ladak, would stop their conversations when they saw him approaching, and Mallinger could read the signs. As is his way, he would slip away without fuss, taking a few months out of the game as he concentrated on fighting the leukaemia, and then, as his health improved, buy his way into local rivals Corby Town. He became chairman of the Southern League club and took Wilson with him as manager and Dunham, Leech and Les Manning as directors.

Wilson had left after the press conference and did not join in the fun on the pitch. Despite Ladak praising him in his statement to the media and insisting that he was an 'integral part of our plans', Wilson drove home more convinced than ever that his time at Kettering was up.

Wilson handed in his resignation five days later. He had been unsure of the financial situation should he quit, but he had no reason to worry. When he did make the decision to leave, Mallinger would write him out a cheque for the money he was due by virtue of the one-year rolling contract he had signed a few months earlier.

He had watched Gascoigne's first game as manager two days after the press conference, a 1–0 league win over Droylsden, from the stands, having been told he was not wanted in the dressing room. The victory had lifted the Poppies to fourth in the table and, in those heady days, a genuine push for promotion seemed inevitable.

Gascoigne put Wilson's nose further out of joint that day by continually talking about 'my players', even though Wilson had brought the majority to the club and spent the best part of the previous two years working to improve them, both individually and as a collective unit.

However, it was an incident that happened before the game that really rankled with Wilson: 'A couple of hours before kick-off I got asked to do an interview with Sky. When I got into the room with them I was told that I was no longer being allowed to do it and that Paul Davis was going to do it instead. Paul Gascoigne had decided that I wasn't to do it. That was his prerogative, but it was over for me. I came in on the Tuesday and told them it wasn't for me.'

Wilson said Ladak tried to talk him into staying, while people whose opinion he valued told him not to be hasty. They pointed to Gascoigne's recent record and told him that, if things didn't work out, then by staying at the club he'd be the right man in the right place to pick up where he had left off. Despite the excitement Gascoigne's appointment had generated, there were still those who felt there was every chance that events in Boston, China and Portugal would repeat themselves here. Mallinger and Leech were among those who preached patience, but Wilson wasn't in the mood to be persuaded otherwise.

His name was rarely mentioned after that by those in charge. Ladak, Gascoigne and Davis had barely got to know the man and their focus was entirely on their big plans. If Wilson didn't want a part of that, it seemed that was his problem alone.

As for the players, some felt uncomfortable at the way in which Wilson had been squeezed out. But there was little they could do about it and the opportunity to play for such a legend, and the potential for full-time wages, meant they were looking at a once-in-a-lifetime opportunity. They were quickly learning that they were the envy of the part-time game and there were plenty of players willing to fill their boots if they wanted to follow Wilson out of the door. At this stage, none did.

This was now the club that everyone below Football League level wanted to play for. Ryan-Zico Black was the first signing of the Gascoigne era, joining the club three weeks into the new regime. He was a young, attacking midfielder contracted to Lancaster Town and could barely contain his excitement when he was told Kettering were prepared to pay £10,000 for him. He drove to the ground and then sold himself short in contract negotiations with Ladak because, 'I was too busy thinking what Gazza would be like.'

Black could not have been happier. He was promised a two-and-a-half-year contract with a basic wage of £20,000 a year that would rise by £5,000 as soon as the playing staff went full-time, which wouldn't be long. He was told the club wanted promotion that season; the Football League was the goal. He and his girlfriend were put up in a five-star spa hotel, where they ordered room service and champagne. At the age of 25, he had hit the big time. Or so it seemed.

As he sweated in the hotel sauna the next morning, he wasn't to know of the power struggle that was already simmering between chairman and manager, and how that was to impact on him. Although Gascoigne, who later accused Ladak of being a 'control freak', had welcomed Black to the club with a kiss, he felt the player had been forced on him by a chairman who, he was soon to allege, wanted too much say in team affairs. And the players already at the club were convinced Black was the chairman's signing.

Within days, Black was to find himself at the centre of growing ill feeling between Gascoigne and Ladak. There was also resentment from his new teammates over his salary and contract. His dream move degenerated into a nightmare. Six months and three managers after the excitement of signing to play for his hero, he'd had his fill of pretty much everybody at Rockingham Road other than a few teammates. He would quit to return to his former club, accepting both part-time football and part-time wages as he looked to put six months of bitter disappointment behind him.

Even then, it was to come with a snag that was to cause him further aggravation, despite moving more than 100 miles away.

*   *   *

Mallinger was able to hand the club over with his head held high. When he had first walked through the doors 12 years earlier, there had been every chance it could go under. Wilson, too, could leave content that he had turned the club's fortunes around on the pitch, having led them into the Conference North. They were fifth in the table, doing well, and he was handing over to Gascoigne a squad of players who were extremely confident of their ability to mount a serious title challenge. Although he was bitterly upset at being pushed aside, he spoke for most people in the room when he said at the press conference, 'If Paul turns out to be as good a manager as he was a player, then he is going to be a very good manager.'

5

FULL-TIME PROFESSIONAL IN A PART-TIME WORLD

BY NOW, Gascoigne was little more than 18 months away from his 40th birthday. If he was to make something of the rest of his life, at least in footballing terms, he needed to prove to himself, more than to anybody else, that he could handle the pressures of management.

He needed Kettering Town just as much as he felt the club needed him. If this project came to nothing, like so many others before it, then it was unlikely anybody would take a gamble on him again, other than perhaps to try to grab a few headlines or put a few bums on seats via Gazza.

As he moved into the manager's office, his new role seemed to invigorate him, giving him a sense of purpose and direction. He took his responsibility for 'my players' seriously. He was keen to be involved in every aspect of the club. He even laughed at himself as 'chief bottle washer', as he explained how he was doing so much more than picking the team and helping Davis run the scattering of training sessions that could be fitted in at a part-time club, playing Saturday/Tuesday/Saturday virtually non-stop.

In the first instance, during his initial burst of enthusiasm, he was the football manager he wanted to be. He enjoyed the banter of the dressing room and was happy to get involved as much as he could in training. He was lapping up his role as father-figure to a squad of players who still couldn't believe all this was happening, even if he quickly found the awkward task of telling some of those players they were dropped more difficult than he had anticipated.

He also wanted to demonstrate his commitment by moving to the area, and told the *Evening Telegraph*, 'I have put in a couple of bids for homes outside Kettering, it's just a matter of finding the time to have a proper look at them. I am looking forward to settling down properly.'

Naturally, he wasn't prepared to reveal where the houses were for fear of the paparazzi, but the talk was of the picturesque villages of Rothwell and Rushton.

Despite all the good intentions, however, semi-professional Kettering Town was a very different environment to the clubs at which he had played at most of his career. The players were not around during daylight hours because they were away doing their regular jobs, and, with only a handful of people at the club during office hours, there was little happening to keep him occupied.

He worked hard to keep himself busy by arranging operations for those players who needed them or by sorting out new boot deals, new match balls, new tracksuits and new diet sheets. He even claimed to have personally stocked up the players' bar with Lucozade.

But what Gascoigne wanted to do most was spend time with his players, and that was not possible. Boredom was a constant menace and Gascoigne had too much spare time on his hands trying to be a consummate full-time professional in a part-time world.

Mallinger reflected insightfully, 'Other than a pub, a

football club must be the worst place in the world for an alcoholic who cannot resist the temptation – the place is full of drink.'

Unfortunately, Gascoigne had the keys to the bar in his pocket.

There is no doubt that he tried hard to keep his addiction under control as he embarked on the adventure. But until he walked into the manager's office he had no first-hand experience of quite how demanding, and lonely, the role can be. While his reputation alone ensured the players, at least initially, were attentive and responsive, they were the least of his early problems at a club which, because of its status, was organised very differently to those he had played for.

While the environment at top clubs is strictly controlled because of the intense pressure from media and fans, in non-League most clubs are relaxed about the dressing room, tunnel area, lounges and mixing with players. Indeed, many of these clubs only survive thanks to a small band of unpaid volunteers whose only reward is to rub shoulders with the players they cheer on every Saturday afternoon. They often take up roles such as kit-men, cleaners, drivers and barmen, and they might even run onto the pitch with a bucket and sponge.

The local paper's football writer will usually hang around the tunnel or in the players' bar, chatting to footballers who are ordinary guys trying to make their mortgage repayments and give their family a few treats by combining a day job with the demands of part-time football. They know the relationship between footballer and journalist can be mutually beneficial: the local paper can be handy when a footballer needs to promote testimonial functions or, if the club get lucky, they find a sponsor who'd appreciate a little publicity in return.

Although Gascoigne has always retained the ability to

relate to, and talk to, ordinary people, he was fiercely protected during his years as the country's top footballer. He was shielded from the media, appointments needed to be made, and much of his time and his commitments were organised by his club or his advisers. This had to be the case, for such were the demands on him that he would never have had time for training or playing, or doing all the demanding physical work needed to recover from his latest injury.

So his first experiences of Rockingham Road's informality both shocked and surprised him. As a serious football manager, he wanted control over who had access to his players. He set about introducing a raft of new rules, dictating who was, and who wasn't, allowed in the dressing room, the tunnel and the directors' lounge, who was allowed to talk to the players and who was to be kept at arm's length. To him, it was the only way a football club could be run. To those who had seen themselves as part of the 'team' but now found themselves unable to talk their way past the new security, it was a snub. Both Gascoigne and Ladak were motivated to make every aspect of Kettering Town as professional as possible, but in that first week the club was as reliant on the selfless volunteers as it always had been.

As Dave Dunham said, because it was Gascoigne people tended to come over all star-struck. Nobody raised their voice. But with a few more noses put out of place, there was the first hint of grumbling, although nobody was yet ready to say, or do, anything which might threaten their place in the new order. To be part of the Gascoigne experience, even from a distance, was something nobody had expected, and they weren't willing to give it up because they could no longer hang around in the tunnel. Anyway, perhaps it would all settle down once the novelty wore off.

But Jon Dunham couldn't wait for that. If he was no longer allowed to wait in the tunnel to grab a few quotes from the players, he'd hang around the car park instead: 'It was such a big story for us, I couldn't let it go. With the players I had to start talking to them wherever I could. Nobody ever said anything to me about not talking to the players, and I never felt the need to ask. I dare say if I had asked his permission he would have said no. But I think he lived in a bubble. I'm not sure how aware he was of anything that wasn't directly affecting him.'

If Gascoigne sensed any resentment, he gave no indication of it. And anyway, he had bigger fish to fry, with his newly-inherited squad of players and a weight of expectation.

Although clubs like Kettering tended to play a large number of midweek matches – apart from 46 league games there are different cup competitions which can take the tally to at least 60 in a typical season – Gascoigne's immediate priority was to get his players in for more training than the one, possibly two, sessions a week which was the norm.

He had spoken to Ladak about bringing in big names, but he seemed to appreciate the honesty and commitment of the majority of players he had inherited. It didn't hurt that some were still rubbing their eyes in disbelief that the 'gaffer' was a footballer who might as well have been beamed down from another planet. He was happy to give them a go as he launched his search for new talent, and, with the help of Davis, saw it as his responsibility to educate them in a better way of playing football than the hoof-and-chase often prevalent at this level of the game.

There had certainly been an element of that until the arrival of Gascoigne and Davis, something which Wilson admits was a necessity. Work-rate and grinding out results were often placed ahead of bringing the ball down and keeping possession. At Conference North level, that was the norm rather than the exception, and training would focus as much on how to impede the opposition as to what you do when you've got the ball at your feet. Especially if you were a defender, whose first responsibility was to get the ball as far away from your own goal as possible.

That wasn't the football that Gascoigne and Davis wanted. In particular, the former Arsenal man, who continued in his role as Football Development Officer at the PFA during his time at Kettering, set out to introduce a whole new philosophy.

Wilson's successes had been built on the pragmatics of managing a group of footballers who trained together for no more than a few hours a week. He wanted his team organised, hard to beat, capable of defending corners and free-kicks, defiant and prepared to run their socks off as they chased the channels and shut the opposition down. He valued character and grit as much as technical ability because it didn't matter how gifted a player was at this level: if he couldn't mix it, then he was going to be bullied out of the game.

From the outset, Gascoigne and Davis insisted the players must take every opportunity to bring the ball down and pass it to each other. They demanded that defenders trust their teammates rather than launch the ball 60 yards upfield. They wanted their goalkeeper rolling the ball out to a full-back occasionally rather than just booting it as far as he could.

Davis spelled out his philosophy when he explained how he employed the methods of his mentor, Arsene Wenger, the Arsenal manager: 'Arsene wants players to express themselves, not be afraid of making mistakes. He doesn't complicate things and the players don't get bored while training. Arsene makes sure all the players see a lot of the ball.'

To help impose the changes, Gascoigne had proposed a two-pronged approach, which Ladak had gone along with: firstly, to sign new players more in tune with the sort of football he wanted to play and, secondly, to take the squad full-time. Players were to be told to give up their day jobs and devote all their time to football or ship out, while Ladak was always happy to scout potential new signings. As the man writing out the cheques, he was also able to back his own judgment by bringing in players he liked, an issue about which Gascoigne was to become increasingly resentful, but at least initially he was able to set his doubts aside.

However, even at this stage there were indications of the problems that lay ahead. Just a week after the press conference to announce his arrival, Gascoigne attended a second one ahead of the FA Cup first-round tie against Stevenage. Quite apart from the fact that two formal press conferences in eight days was in itself unique, there were notable differences in Gascoigne's demeanour.

With fewer journalists present – this time it just about reached double figures – this conference was shifted to a corner of the social club. Those reporters who did attend were introduced, as they walked in, to a small group representing boot sponsors. The journalists from the national media did no more than walk by to take their seats, ready to ask Gascoigne another load of questions about pretty much everything he had talked about the previous week, but the local guys felt obliged to pass a few minutes chatting to the PR team. Billingham, hovering nearby, expected the deal to be the first of many.

The top table was laid out pretty much the same as the previous week, save for the prominent placement of a pair of the new boots and a ball. This time Gascoigne sat alone. The plaster that had covered his neck had gone, but his body language was less open and more challenging. Veritably a fidget, he initially sat rigid, with arms folded and eyes staring straight ahead. After a couple of soft questions he began rhythmically slapping his left shoulder with his right hand.

His answers were shorter and sharper, and it was clear when he sat down to do a couple of one-on-ones, or two-on-ones, that he was preoccupied.

Whatever the cause of his anxiety that day, it was the press that bore the brunt of his mood. He ranted against *The Sun* newspaper for running a sweepstake on how long his Kettering career would last. He then turned his attention to a leading bookmaker, which had been offering odds of 6–1 that he would be gone by Christmas, saying this was typical of a cynical clique's attitude to everything he did.

'I don't know them, but I just knew what was going to be said,' he said. 'I told the lads to get prepared, you are going to be in the spotlight from now on regardless of who you are. From now on, as long as I'm around, you're going to be in the headlines.'

He insisted he would deal with the cynics by ignoring them, but that was something he seemed incapable of doing. The criticism – mild as it was compared to some he had endured over the previous decade, and which no doubt the paper and bookmaker felt was just a bit of fun – touched a nerve. When I asked him how he handled it, he railed, 'I've been coping with it for 23 years. The World Cup in 1990, that was manic, when you get divorced that was manic, when you're in the courtrooms that was manic, it's just something you have to deal with.

'I know I can deal with things because I've been in the game for 23 years. There's just times when I have to laugh it off, or sometimes switch my phone off and leave it off for the day.

'Everything I do is positive. It's just unfortunate that people write lies and wrong things. I'm the first to hold my hands up when I've done something wrong. You don't have to go round putting lies about me. If I'm wrong I'll put my hands up and admit it.'

While Gascoigne ranted, Ladak and Billingham were busy drawing up their plans to propel the club forward as quickly as possible. Their business plan assumed greatly increased attendances for matches in the wake of the hysteria whipped up by Gazzamania, and they sent out a call for more stewards and gatemen to handle the expected rush. Plans were drawn up for a fundraising 'Evening with Paul Gascoigne' at the nearby Wicksteed Park Pavilion a couple of weeks before Christmas, prices from £400 for tables of 10. The main money-spinners were the three VIP tables at £1,000 plus VAT each, which came with pre-dinner drinks with celebrities, complimentary photographs and tables in a prime location. Former England striker and Wolves legend Steve Bull, represented by Billingham, was announced as the first special guest, and there was the promise of more to come.

Ladak and Billingham started to make contact with local businesses. Doors which had been firmly shut on Mallinger and his team over the previous years were magically opened at the mention of Gascoigne's name. Even people with limited interest in, or knowledge of, football seemed to have an affinity with the fallen hero. They were ready to explore ways of getting up close and personal with the man who had played such a big part in revitalising the appeal of a sport which had been pretty much in disgrace because of football hooliganism and tragedies such as Bradford, Heysel and Hillsborough.

Gascoigne's tears at the 1990 World Cup, and his ability to make people laugh with him, played a big part in changing attitudes. The late Bobby Robson, his national team boss in his formative years, had described him as 'daft as a brush'. The gloom that had fallen on football began to lift, and there is no doubt that Gascoigne was a catalyst. Even Prime Minister Margaret Thatcher, who had treated football with barely concealed contempt, saw the advantages in opening the doors of No. 10 to Gazza and the returning 'heroes'. The fact that England had again been knocked out of a major tournament by the Germans seemed to have been washed away by Gascoigne's tears.

For many football fans, in Kettering just as much as any other town in the country, these were defining moments in their football psyche. So it was understandable that when he turned up in their little market town they wanted to be a part of it. It really was something to get worked up about.

'The opportunity for the club to make the most of Paul was obvious and we had shirts with an "8" and "Gazza" printed on the back,' said Mallinger. 'They sold like hot cakes and our problem was getting supplies through quickly enough. Suddenly everybody wanted to be seen wearing a Kettering Town shirt and the phone lines between our kit manufacturers, Vandanel, and ourselves were red hot.'

'I Scored at Rockingham Road' knickers went on sale at £3 a pair.

It wasn't only dedicated Poppies fans or those who suddenly discovered the football club after Gascoigne's arrival who wanted a piece of the action. Mallinger recalls one telephone call to the club in which a man asked if Gascoigne would call in at a dinner party he was hosting with his wife on a forthcoming Saturday evening. Mallinger said, 'They weren't football supporters but they thought it would be a way to impress their guests.' Gascoigne laughed off that particular invite, although his behaviour could be so unpredictable it would not have been a complete surprise had he knocked on their door.

6

ALREADY FEELING THE STRAIN

BY FAR the biggest frustration for Peter Mallinger during his time as chairman was the issue of the ground. Rockingham Road is well past its sell-by date and at the start of the 2005/06 season it had failed a safety check, meaning emergency work had to be carried out on part of the main stand. It was the latest plaster-and-paint repair job at a stadium with a limited future.

Diehard fans of the non-League game will describe it as a 'real' football ground, which basically means it is three-quarters terracing. Both ends are uncovered, with the Cowper Street End backing onto the rear gardens of a row of terraced houses that offer a free view of games from the upstairs window. The away end backs on to Rockingham Road itself, separated by a row of trees. On the opposite side to the main stand is the partly-covered Britannia Road Terrace. Everybody recognises that the stadium's best days probably belonged to the 1950s.

Very little has changed over the years. Scope for redevelopment is limited by the nature of the surrounding housing and roads; the club do not own the land on which they play; despite years of discussions there had been little progress over either improving the ground or moving to a new site; and the landlord seemed determined to run down a lease due to expire in 2013. Kettering, identified in government plans as an area for major urban growth, has seen a large amount of housing development in recent decades, and it seems almost inevitable that in the not-too-distant future houses and apartments will stand on land which once hosted a football club.

When Gascoigne and Ladak arrived at Rockingham Road, the mantra was that they were going to bust a gut to get Kettering Town into the Football League. But just because Kettering had never made it up there with the big boys, that didn't mean the club was quite as minor-league as some tried to portray it. Relegation on the last day of the 2000/01 season ended a run of 30 consecutive years in the top flight of non-League football; seven years prior to the takeover they had almost made it into the Football League, when they finished runners-up to Cheltenham Town in the Conference in 1998/99. They finished that season four points behind the Robins (as Cheltenham are known) and four points ahead of Rushden & Diamonds in fourth place. Unfortunately, that was the pinnacle.

The club did enjoy a day out at Wembley for the 2000 FA Trophy final, which they lost 3–2 to Kingstonian, but they slipped quickly and suffered relegation a year later. To rub salt into the wounds, Diamonds won promotion to the Football League as Conference champions that season – the upstart neighbours who hadn't existed a decade earlier were now top dog.

Back in 1974, Kettering had come close to election to the Football League in the days when club chairmen voted on relegation and promotion issues. They missed out by just five votes, as the League clubs again looked after their own in a way that eventually prompted the scrapping of the old pals' act. Automatic promotion from the top tier of the non-League game was introduced.

And even if none of their previous managers had been as big a name as Paul Gascoigne, there had been Tommy Lawton, Derek Dougan, Ron Atkinson and Graham Carr. Lawton had won 23 full England caps and 23 wartime caps in a sparkling playing career interrupted by the Second World War; Dougan was a Wolverhampton Wanderers and Northern Ireland legend of the 1960s and 1970s; Atkinson went on to manage the likes of West Bromwich Albion, Manchester United and Atletico Madrid; and Carr, father of TV comic Alan Carr, went on to manage League clubs such as Northampton Town and Blackpool, before carving out a good reputation as a scout for the likes of Tottenham Hotspur and Manchester City. Gascoigne certainly wasn't following in the footsteps of a bunch of nobodies.

Although attendances had faded away to average just over 900 in those first few games of 2005/06, the consortium reckoned there was potential. The average crowd for the 1998/99 season had been 2,032, and they felt Gascoigne's presence would help them get close to that without too much fuss. A quick surge into the Football League would improve it further.

However, something had to be done about the ground. The Football League has rules covering leaseholds, and Kettering could have won every game in their first two years under Gascoigne and still not made it to the promised land. While it was exciting to hear talk of a full-time squad, new signings and a reserve team, without the ground issue being resolved there was no hope outside the non-League game.

Insiders say that Ladak and Gascoigne were not aware of the potential minefield that was the lease until after they began talks to buy the club. They resolved to not let it stand in their way, and backed themselves to succeed where Mallinger had failed in getting things moving. Ladak was more hopeful that his fresh presence would help soften attitudes, and Mallinger believed that Gascoigne's name could help overcome the ill-feeling between Kettering Borough Council and the club.

'We had no help from Kettering Borough Council, none whatsoever,' said Mallinger. 'There were all sorts of ideas involving supermarkets and the Duke of Buccleuch estate. We had some really good ideas. The council just threw them out, they weren't interested. I always had the feeling that they'd have far sooner we'd gone bust and they could have locked the gates and said we haven't got a football club in Kettering because we don't want one.'

Ladak was hopeful that a fresh approach would herald results: 'Obviously we need the support of the council. I am really hoping that they will back the club and back the team. If we are going to play League football, then everyone knows we need a new stadium. It is one of our main priorities. I believe the fan base is there at the club but we need the stadium and facilities to match it.'

The one reason why anybody around the club believed Ladak might stand a better chance than Mallinger in making progress was Gascoigne. Even non-footballing people were fascinated by him. 'When Gascoigne got involved, suddenly there'd be letters and requests coming through from the borough council asking if the manager could attend this and that function, whether he'd switch on the Christmas lights that autumn and so on and so on,' said Mallinger. 'We'd never been asked anything like that before. So, yes, suddenly the borough council did start paying a bit more attention to the football club. I think even they realised they had got a star among them. Maybe if he'd stayed a bit longer they might have been able to work something out.'

Chris Smith-Haynes, a social worker, had been elected as the Conservative councillor for the All Saints ward covering Rockingham Road two years prior to Gascoigne's arrival. She said the council was committed to helping the football club find a new stadium, but she was aware relationships weren't what they could be. She also felt the arrival of Gascoigne could help create opportunities to look forward together, rather than hark on about the past.

In her early forties and with a lifelong association with the town, she said the club's future lay away from the built-up area. 'Of course we wanted the football club to have a suitable site. However, we are governed by guidelines and regulations, and perhaps people expected more than we could give them. The football club is a privately owned company and we couldn't get financially involved with it any more than we could with Marks & Spencer.'

However, the talk in the wake of the takeover was encouraging. There was a chance for greater co-operation and Smith-Haynes got on the telephone to invite Gascoigne to the Civic Ball at Wicksteed Park that November. She didn't receive a reply.

Not to be discouraged, she was pleased to learn he had agreed to switch on the Christmas lights in the town centre: 'I was in the crowd cheering him,' she recalls. 'That showed he wanted good relations between the club and the town. To me, there was a glimmer of hope and I felt we should go for it. Unfortunately, he was only there a few more days after that.'

One problem for Ladak – as he tried to put together plans to either purchase the leasehold or, more likely, move the club to a new site – was that he needed Gascoigne to open doors, but could not control what his manager either did or said.

During one pre-match briefing early on, Gascoigne was talking with enthusiasm about all the different ideas he had – by this time the plans had grown to include a training ground away from Rockingham Road – when he told me that the club was in competition with supermarket giant Tesco for land.

He was excited by the plans, which he felt showed how far the club had come. But Ladak was furious. He knew the damage that could be done when negotiations were not kept under wraps. He was upset with the *Evening Telegraph* for reporting what Gascoigne had said beneath the banner headline 'It's Tesco v Poppies', while Billingham tried to claim that what Gascoigne had said was off the record. I told them that at no time in the course of that interview had anything been said about it not being for use in the paper. If it had, there would have been no question of my putting it in. I even offered to play back the tape.

The next time I met Gascoigne he threw in an 'off-the-record' joke about Tesco, obviously having been told about how our previous conversation had caused concern. I liked the way he handled it, with humour rather than drama, which only reinforced what the players had been saying about him in those early days trying to manage them with a smile, at least in training.

Ladak continued to explore ways to find the club a more suitable site, and there was talk about moving in with one of the neighbouring minor-league clubs. Gascoigne, meanwhile, made sure that progress towards full-time professionalism stayed on the front burner. 'I'd like everyone to have in their mind that they would like to become professional football players, and that's the response I've had off them,' he said.

Unfortunately, he was still not seeing enough of those players and he continued to try to find ways to keep himself busy. 'I've been ringing up the guys who are injured and some of them have been waiting nine months for an operation,' he said. 'I've got them having it done next week. I've done every job you can think of in this club from the tea man up. Next step is probably cleaning the stands. I've been getting boots for my players, making sure they now have pasta, pizzas and chicken after training, stocking up with Lucozade, everything that I had as a professional.'

Although a list of transfer targets had been drawn up, Gascoigne was content for now to work with the players he had inherited. He enjoyed those moments when he had their full attention: 'The lads have been great, and there's been a lot of banter. I've had stick from my players about my shoes.'

The dressing room had been solid under Wilson, but even in the early days of the new regime there were concerns. 'Gazza was one of my boyhood heroes; when I was growing up he was one of the best players in the world,' says Christian Moore. 'Before he arrived we had a settled squad, the manager was doing well, the club was doing well and so you thought, what was going to change? Especially when you heard that Les Ferdinand and Darren Anderton and every other person of that level was to be coming in. You couldn't help but think, "Am I going to be got rid of?"'

Brett Solkhon also began to question whether he had a future: 'He said he'd give everyone a chance, but there were a lot of rumours that he was going to sign players like Les Ferdinand and Steve McManaman. It was in the back of my mind that I might be leaving as a result of people like that coming in.

'I was telling myself how good it would be to be involved with a club where all this was happening. Just to be around someone like Gascoigne was huge. Some of us even thought we might get to play alongside him in the team.'

While Gascoigne talked about offering as many as 12 players a full-time contract, he wanted to add to a squad that had, like many clubs at this level, been functioning without a reserve team. As Mallinger pointed out, a second string was expensive and there was not a lot of evidence to suggest they were great value for money: 'It's a matter of whether or not you've got the money to do it. It's not cheap. We had two or three occasions when we had a reserve side at Kettering, and then a couple of years later we'd disband it because it proved expensive and the managers weren't getting much benefit from it other than the odd player who was coming back from injury. At the end of the day at this level, managers tend to say if we want a player we'll get one from another club.'

But nothing was going to stand in the way of the new regime's quest for bigger and better things, and Gascoigne knew what he wanted. 'I need to strengthen the squad and make it bigger. When you add in the youngsters we have got a squad of around 27. But we've got four out injured, so that's 23. Then we've got three apprentices so that leaves 20. Then we've got three keepers so that's 17. And we need 11 players and five subs.'

Gascoigne was not going to put his hand in his pocket to finance the plans. That burden had fallen on Ladak, and it was going to be expensive. Mallinger had tried to cut costs over the preceding few years and the wage bill had been slashed from £408,809 in 2001 to £228,866 the year before he sold up. While this had helped reduce the six-figure losses being reported at the turn of the century, the club still made a loss of £31,231 in the financial year ending June 2004. And Ladak was committed to a massive increase in spending on all the things he and Gascoigne were talking about.

Whatever was happening off the pitch that autumn, few doubted the team's ability to make a decent push for promotion. November may have started with defeat by Stevenage, but it was followed by the best performance under Gascoigne, the 4–1 drubbing of Stalybridge Celtic that had him roaring, 'This club is really going places.'

Stalybridge boss John Reed was in his 26th year of non-League management. He acknowledged his side had been taken apart by a team he felt was going to walk away with the title. He described the Kettering football as 'absolutely fantastic' and said, 'I had other managers ringing me up after that game asking what they were like and I told them they were unplayable, it was like they had three extra men. At this level, you don't get the sort of football they played that day.'

Yet there were to be no more League wins under Gascoigne. It might have been only his second League game, and his second victory, but 14 days into his time as a serious football manager this was as good as it was going to get.

Because of their FA Cup commitments, Kettering had dropped to sixth in the table. Not that anybody could have predicted what was to come. They had games in hand and Gascoigne was in his element: 'That's two League games I've picked the team and we've won both.' Despite only having had three training sessions with the squad, he said, 'The players are already learning and will get better,' and he again talked up the togetherness which was so important to him: 'We have an unbelievable team spirit in the dressing room, and I'm so proud of all of them. I couldn't be more pleased.'

Despite the encouraging talk, Gascoigne's doubts about his relationship with Ladak were playing on his mind. When asked the seemingly simple question of whether he would be fielding the same starting line-up for the game two days later against Hednesford, he snapped, 'These are my players, it's my team, my club and now it's my town. I'm going to live here and no one is going to kick me out of my house.' It was a revealing answer, but one which bore absolutely no relation to the questioned posed.

However, he wasn't yet to be distracted. He announced that training was to be increased to three sessions a week from mid-November. The first reserve-team friendly was scheduled for 23 November, away to Stafford Rangers. He also revealed that those players offered a full-time contract would start on 30 January 2006, with a squad of 11 to 18 full-timers named by the end of December. Those not offered a contract but who he wanted to keep at the club would train three evenings a week and still be part of the squad.

Following his neck operation, Gascoigne had been warned by surgeons that the simple act of heading a football too early could be enough to paralyse him. However, his recovery had gone well and a fortnight into his reign he was talking of getting his boots on. He had been told by his doctor following the operation, 'not to lift anything heavier than a coffee cup,' but was now starting to look forward to getting out on the pitch to help Davis with the training. 'It'll be nice to join in with the players. But in my situation I won't be able to play for another three months. That leaves a few months until the end of the season, and if my players are good enough there's no need for me to play.'

When asked what he felt about playing at a level of football where clattering into Paul Gascoigne would be seen as something of a trophy, he retorted, 'I've seen the players in this league, and I can look after myself.'

Perhaps so. But whether he could look after himself off the pitch – as the pressure of management put a strain on his health and his ability to resist alcohol – was another matter. The well-respected Scottish manager Walter Smith had long taken a fatherly interest in Gascoigne, having managed him during some fantastically successful years at Glasgow Rangers in the 1990s, and he was well qualified to advise Gazza about the pitfalls and pressures of the job.

And it seemed Gascoigne was beginning to feel the strain when he admitted after just two weeks, 'I'm not having enough time on what I want at the moment because I'm too busy trying to organise Kettering Town Football Club the way I want it run. It's coming together now, although it has been non-stop. Walter Smith did tell us that management would be tough. I said, "Yeah, yeah," but he was right. I suppose if you walked into a top Premiership club you've got all this ready for you. But here I'm looking at everything. The only peace I get is on a Saturday for 90 minutes with my players.'

Gascoigne relied heavily on Davis. His assistant manager often picked him up from Champneys and returned him at odd hours. Davis was also responsible for training, although he had to work harder to make an impression on the players. 'Everyone knows Gazza but Paul Davis was a new name to me,' said Andy Hall, who was only nine years old when Davis played his last game for Arsenal.

A lot of the pressure Gascoigne was experiencing was self-imposed, and after a hectic first two weeks he admitted he was finding it an 'intense' experience. 'I have to look at teams, I have to look at videos, I have to look at my team and watch them in training. I have to do all the things that a manager does. As long as I keep acting as a professional off the field, then I'll expect my players to act that way on the field.'

Drawing on the experiences that had caused him so much heartache, he revealed, 'I told them to make sure they're doing the right things on and off the field because they will get followed. And I will get to find out about them. They say a young fox can't kid an old one and I've tried all those tricks.'

Even as he spoke, the relationship between him and many of his players was shifting. Players who had been star-struck on Gascoigne's appointment were smelling alcohol on his breath and there were rumours of his drinking in the boardroom and sponsors' lounge. They had also seen bottles of wine on the coach to away games. Some of the respect he had been afforded simply for being Gazza was being chipped away. Even at this stage, a few were questioning whether it would last.

None of this had become a big issue, it was more something to giggle about between themselves. It only took on greater significance when viewed alongside their other growing concerns: team selections they didn't agree with, changes to tactics and formations, the offer of contracts to some players but not to others, mundane training sessions, the introduction of new players many felt weren't as good as those already there, and the treatment of a couple of key men in the dressing room.

One popular player would be driven out of the club and another left an answerphone message telling him he was no longer welcome. Both had strong allies in the squad and other players would not be happy with the way their mates were treated. It seemed team spirit and morale would be next to leave the club.

7

PLAY LIKE YOU'RE WORLD CUP WINNERS!

WELL before Paul Gascoigne appeared on the scene, the players had been convinced that 2005/06 was to be their season. As they gathered for pre-season training in the summer, they were confident they could build on their fourth-place finish a few months earlier in the inaugural Conference North season. Despite lacking firepower, they qualified for the divisional play-off semi-final and saw off Droylsden before losing a cracking final 3–2 to Altrincham, who went on to take their place in the Conference.

Wilson had them back early that summer and worked hard on improving fitness. He also signed a trio of strikers with excellent reputations: Christian Moore, Neil Midgley and Junior McDougald. Moore started out with Leicester City and Stockport County and had made a big name for himself in the non-League game. In 1993, Telford United paid a club record £20,000 fee to take him from Conference rivals Burton Albion, a club he ended up playing for in three different spells. Just as important as his goals were his experience and reputation as a big character, something

Wilson valued in his players. Midgley, a product of the youth academy at Ipswich Town, made his way to Rockingham Road via a free-scoring spell at Barnet and Canvey Island, and McDougald had come through the Tottenham youth system to play nearly 300 times for the likes of Brighton, Rotherham and Dagenham & Redbridge.

Wilson had worked hard on making his side difficult to beat, and they were defensively sound. But he introduced the new strikers to rectify a lack of goals that had seen them score just 56 in 42 league games the previous season.

Right-back Wayne Diuk, who had been at the club for six full seasons, had ridden the rollercoaster highs and lows of the previous few years, involving promotion, relegation and a spell when the club was in such trouble that the players went months without pay. He believed Wilson had assembled a squad of ability and character that would mount a serious assault on the title. He had been promised a testimonial and was looking forward to a good season for both the club and himself.

'Kev got us in early and brought in these proven strikers, which was just what we needed,' he recalls. 'Every player who started that season says if all the Gazza stuff hadn't gone on we would have won that league. We played well in pre-season and Kev really pushed us hard. He didn't like the way we had lost the play-off the season before and I really believed we were going to win the league. The squad had improved and the team spirit was the best I'd played in, even better than when we won the league.'

Kettering had won the Dr Martens League Premier Division title in 2001/02 to reclaim their place in the Conference, but an almost inevitable relegation followed 12 months later as the club finished 14 points adrift at the bottom.

Like Wilson, Diuk, a nippy defender who had been on the books of Notts County as a teenager, felt they had plenty of big characters. He points to the likes of centre-half and captain Derek Brown – 'the nicest guy in the world off the pitch but on the pitch just scary' – Jamie Paterson, Christian Moore, Craig McIlwain and David Theobald: 'Everyone really, we just gelled well and had a very good changing room.'

Wilson had employed former England and Arsenal defender Nigel Winterburn to help coach his defence, and the instructions were clear.

'Every training session he'd come in and take the back four and the other defenders in the squad and work us,' says Diuk. 'It was all about the basics. He told me as a full-back that my job was to cover the centre-half and if he didn't head it then I had to clear it. That was it. He said that's how George Graham used to train them. If you can get forward, then fair enough, but your job was to stop the other side scoring. George Graham told him he had the Arsenal fans singing his name by getting him to kick the ball out of the ground.'

The season started promisingly. Six games into their league campaign, Kettering were unbeaten in second place. Three games without a win, including their first defeat of the season at Northwich Victoria, saw them drop to ninth on 1 October, but they bounced back. By the time the team was handed over to Gascoigne, Kettering had gone five games without conceding a goal and were back up to fifth. And they had played less games than many of their rivals as a result of the FA Cup run that took them into the first round proper, a big occasion for non-League footballers.

'We didn't look like conceding, we were so solid,' says Diuk. 'Everyone knew their job and if you didn't do it then you got told in no uncertain terms. It wasn't a case of, "Can you do that a bit better, please?" You got a rollicking. Getting a rollicking off the manager, it's not the same as when your mates turn round and tell you to sort yourself out. That wakes you up.'

Wilson had been delighted with the way his plan had come together, and was naturally devastated to find his own position under threat. He felt he had a squad capable of taking the club to promotion, and a bunch of lads who were easy to manage. 'They dealt with things sometimes before I got in the dressing room at half-time. They would argue because there were strong personalities in Mark Osborn, Jamie Paterson, Darren Lynch, Derek Brown, Craig McIlwain, Diuky and Christian Moore, and sometimes there'd be punch-ups. Things that needed saying were often said before I got my chance, and I think it hurts more when it comes from your own teammates. They were a strong squad, united, and they all felt they were capable of getting on.'

Wilson felt the new management's best option would be to let things carry on pretty much as they were. The team was on a roll and the players were busting a gut to prove to Gascoigne they were worth their place.

None of the players had met Gascoigne face-to-face before he appeared in the dressing room ahead of the Droylsden game, although all had received a call from him the day before. They answered their phone to find Paul Davis asking for them by name before handing it over to Gascoigne. He said pretty much the same to all the players: 'I'm looking forward to meeting you all tomorrow and wishing you all the best.'

One player, believing it to be a wind-up, swore at Davis and hung up. Only when Davis rang back and Gascoigne took the phone did he accept it was genuine.

Andy Hall was 19 years old when he got his call. He had completed a three-year YTS scheme with Coventry City before being released and was trying to make it as a footballer while working in a factory. 'When someone rings you up and says Paul Gascoigne wants to talk to you, you've got to think it might be one of your mates winding you up,' he said. 'He said people had told him about me, that I was a good player and I was going to be a big part of his team. Coming from someone like him ... well, it was a privilege.'

The squad met in the dressing room as usual before the game, but the buzz was quieter. Nobody knew what to expect, and they waited anxiously for Gascoigne to make his appearance. When he walked through the door an hour before kick-off, some struggled to mask their surprise. 'The person I remember seeing on TV compared to the guy standing before me, I could have sworn it was a different bloke,' said Diuk.

Moore recalls, 'He was shaking. To most of the lads he was a hero but it was like he had no confidence, he was shy, he was very nervous. I wanted to give him a hug and say, "Come on, you're Paul Gascoigne, you don't need to be nervous here."'

Gascoigne walked round the dressing room to shake the hand of each player and give them a kiss on the cheek. He read out the team but in such hushed tones some of the players were uncertain whether they had been named. There were some quizzical looks before Davis spoke. He told them he knew they played a certain way but, 'We'll get this game out of the way,' and things would start to change.

Davis's comments were not universally welcome, and some players felt they were being put down. They were full of confidence on the back of their bright start to the season and had respected Wilson's no-nonsense approach. Behind the hype and excitement of Gascoigne's arrival, some wondered what he and Davis actually knew about football at their level.

'We did clear our lines quickly, but when we got in the final third we could still play a bit,' said Diuk.

The players had also been taken aback by just how nervous Gascoigne was, although Jamie Paterson helped ease the tension. With a reputation as the team joker, the Scot got the first laugh by poking fun at Gascoigne's expensive white shoes. Then, as Gascoigne went to leave, he asked him to press 'play' on the CD machine by the door. As Gascoigne did so, his own awful version of 'Fog on the Tyne' blared out. The dressing room erupted. Gascoigne laughed with them before heading off to the boardroom for a glass of wine.

'Paul's preparation for every game was straight on the wine followed in half-an-hour by a request for the brandy,' says Mallinger, who was in the boardroom for each of the home games when Gascoigne was manager. 'Every game was the same. He would come into the boardroom to drink it straight but if he went to his office he would send a plastic cup of coffee down for Barbara [Mallinger's wife] to add top-ups.'

Nothing about the day was normal. As the players ran out of the tunnel, they were greeted by a wall of photographers, whereas for most games there would be one, maybe two. 'We were all a bit nervous,' says Diuk. 'Droylsden were a good side. We beat them in the play-offs the year before and they were pushing again. I remember starting the game and completely missing the ball. I thought to myself, "What am I doing here?" A couple of the lads did as well.'

The nerves gradually faded. Although the game was goalless at half-time, the players felt they had acquitted themselves well once things had settled down. Gascoigne said little other than offering a few words of encouragement, and Christian Moore came off the bench to score the only goal from a cross by Diuk, who was made man of the match.

Gascoigne stuck his head round the dressing-room door to say 'well done' to the players before heading off to meet the media. Diuk was later called to the sponsors' lounge to be presented with his award by Gascoigne. He also got a kiss on the cheek. 'That was the last any of us saw of him that day,' said Diuk. 'My girlfriend was there and it was back in the car and off we went. I had mates texting me to say it had come up on *Final Score* that I'd put the ball across for the goal. I drove home thinking, "Hang on a minute, this is Conference North ... what's happening?"'

If the introduction to Gascoigne and Davis had been a disappointingly low-key and nervous affair for the players, they found out who was in charge when they headed to the ground the following Tuesday for training. Paul Davis ran the show with a flip chart detailing dos and don'ts.

The first rule was not to talk to the media without permission, which the players felt was to protect Gascoigne. Wilson had let them talk to the local paper or radio without a second thought, and the conversation would invariably be about matters on the pitch. If not, it was only likely to be a few quotes about an injury or a forthcoming game, nothing controversial. But now the players were caught up in something far, far bigger.

Moore had almost fallen off his chair when they were advised, in all seriousness, what to do if they were followed by scandal-sheet journalists when out on the town. 'We were told that if we had any trouble with the newspapers over girls in nightclubs then we were to go to them straight away because they knew people who'd be able to help keep it quiet. I'm married, but do you really think if I was out with a girl it's going to be *Sun* front-page material? I don't think the *News of the World* was going to be paying out money for a picture of me in a nightclub. It was proof of the totally different world they lived in.'

'Suddenly we were reading papers like *The Sun* and seeing headlines,' said Diuk. 'It was a totally different world, and it was all a bit "rabbit in headlights". None of us had had anything like that before. Sure, we were used to playing in front of not-bad crowds, but doing TV interviews and people ringing you up from the papers? All of a sudden we'd got the life of Premier League footballers.'

As Davis turned the pages of his flip chart, the players were told how he wanted them to play. He covered fitness levels, diet, dress code, training and told them not to go out 24 hours ahead of matches. Much of it was what they already knew, and some of the players, having already done a full day's work, struggled to stifle a yawn. They wanted to get outside and start kicking a ball around. Instead, they were led off to the sponsors' lounge, where Davis played a video of the 1998 World Cup final between France and Brazil. He showed a clip of the French back four passing the ball between themselves without a Brazil player in sight and pointed to the players on the TV screen. He told the bemused part-timers this was how they were going to start playing.

'We were watching the likes of Lizarazu, Desailly, Thuram and whoever else winning the World Cup final for France and he was telling us that was how we were going to play,' remembers Diuk. 'It was a bit embarrassing. Obviously they hadn't watched the Conference North much because you just don't get time like that. Basically, it's just 22 people running round like headless chickens. He had a stick and was pointing at the TV saying, "This is what you have to do." We're sitting there thinking, "Has he seen us play yet?"'

The players felt that Gascoigne and Davis had no understanding of football at their level.

'I sat watching the telly and he's telling me I've got to play like Zinedine Zidane,' says Moore, a battering ram of a forward. 'I looked at Jamie Paterson and started laughing. That's when I thought, "This isn't going to work." You've got respect for them because they've played at the highest level, but this was Conference North. This wasn't Wembley Stadium or the Emirates.'

If the players were relieved to finally get outside, they were to find nothing in their world remained untouched. Davis wanted them to immediately start work on their new passing game à la France 1998. It was to begin with the back four. This had typically been Diuk at right back, Derek Brown and Craig McIlwain in the centre of defence and Liam Nicell or Jamie Gould at left-back, and even those players admitted their talents lay more in presenting a solid front: head it away, kick it away and kick the opposition as well, if you could get away with it.

Now they had to implement a style of play that was foreign to them. You no longer kicked the ball long, but passed it along the back four or to a midfield player, even if you were being shut down. To ram home the message, Davis organised a short-sided game in which the only rule was that the ball stayed on the grass. After a couple of minutes of scrappy play, on-loan Hugh McAuley, one of the most naturally gifted players, dinked the ball over an outstretched leg. Davis whistled a halt. 'Keep the ball on the floor,' he ordered McAuley, who replied that if he'd done that the opposing player would have got it. But Davis was insistent.

'That's where things started to change,' says Diuk. 'How we had been successful went out of the window. There was to be no argument. It was to be their way or the highway.'

The training was on a pitch that was heavily overused, and that didn't help. 'You couldn't do what they wanted with the pitches we had to play on,' says Solkhon. 'The ball is always in the air because the pitches are just terrible.'

Midgley, playing without a contract and desperate to impress, recalls, 'It was really basic passing drills, which at that stage of the season was quite mundane. You might do that in pre-season to get used to the ball again but not in November. They kept telling us we were good players but they didn't know where to start with us. You could tell Paul Davis hadn't coached at the level we were playing at. He didn't know where to put us in terms of ability. Does he treat us as he would an under-14 team or an academy team or does he treat us as if he were coaching a Championship or Premiership side? I think he went for the low option and it wasn't a fun thing to do, it was repetitive.

'We were part-time players coming in after a day's work. We had established ourselves at that level. We had Christian Moore and Jamie Paterson and Derek Brown, guys in their 30s, and you're teaching them to suck eggs.'

Moore had been wound up by Davis getting his name wrong. He felt training was, 'very much out of the coaching manual for under-10s,' and that Davis was talking to him as if he was a five-year-old. He didn't enjoy it: 'It didn't help that he called me Derek Brown for the first two sessions. I turned round and told him, "I'm not fucking Derek Brown." You're thinking to yourself, These guys don't even know who you are. They've not made a conscious effort to get to know your name. How was anything supposed to work if they didn't even know the names of their players? They didn't have a clue about the players they were working with.'

While Davis ran training, Gascoigne flitted around the edges. He was far more relaxed than the man who had mumbled his way through the team sheet on Saturday. 'He was a totally different person to what he was on the Saturday,' recalled Diuk. 'He was having a laugh and a joke, it was the Gazza you'd see on TV. He was telling us stories about his England days, things like how Chris Woods had been the most unfit footballer he had ever trained with. One minute he'd be in the dug-out having a fag, then he'd be in the stand having another, then he'd turn up right behind you. I don't think he ever stayed still.'

Photographer Mike Capps made a point of attending as many training sessions as he could. He knew pictures of the England legend kicking a ball could be worth a few bob, and even if he couldn't get them he was a keen Tottenham fan thrilled to be in the company of the maestro who had shot down Arsenal in the 1991 FA Cup semi-final, with a sensational 35-yard free-kick. He occasionally sat with Gascoigne in the dug-out to watch training: 'At first talking to him was hard because it was like there was a brick wall. He thought everybody was out to fleece him or take the piss. But once you got past that stage it was like you became his mate. He'd talk about anything. He cracked me up with the stories he told me of his childhood in Gateshead or as a footballer.

'He wasn't the same guy he had been at Spurs, that was for sure. I was shocked at how thin he was. He couldn't do a lot of training because of his neck, but when he did kick a ball you'd see straight away how much better he was than everyone else.'

Davis had tested the players' patience with his list of dos and don'ts at that first training session and insisted that everything was to be as professional as possible. That included their diets. The players were surprised when Gascoigne, who had disappeared down the tunnel, reappeared to shout, 'The pizzas are here!' He had sent out for £100 worth of pizzas and garlic bread, and training ended with him sending the players inside to tuck in. As they did, Gascoigne told them if it was good enough for Serie A it was good enough for them. It became a regular feature of training during his time.

The players appreciated the gesture, but many would eat the pizzas and then go home to have their dinner – although, for the likes of Midgley and David Theobald, who shared a car from Cambridge, it meant they no longer had to stop at a service station on the A14 on the way home.

That first week was one of only two during the Gascoigne era in which Kettering did not have a scheduled midweek match. Despite the 'luxury' of training sessions on both Tuesday and Thursday, the players felt it was going to take a long time to adapt to the radically different playing style.

For the first time that season, a few were looking ahead to the next match with nagging doubts in the back of their minds. They were also feeling the pressure of all the media attention. It was no longer just a matter of going out and doing a well-rehearsed job for the team and the gaffer. With the BBC cameras on their way for the biggest game of the season, the FA Cup tie with Stevenage, some were unsure whether they had it in them to give up all they had been comfortable with and replace it with a non-League version of total football.

Although the plan was to replicate France's passing game, the players, and many supporters, found it odd that Gascoigne named a centre-half, David Theobald, in the centre of midfield against a Stevenage side going well in the division above them. Ollie Burgess, a former Northampton Town player highly rated by his teammates, found himself on the bench as one of three changes, although at least the back four of Diuk, Brown, McIlwain and Nicell had a familiar look to it.

Stevenage were by far the better team, and the Kettering players admitted they had been lucky to get away with only a 3–1 defeat. 'They had seen all the razzmatazz around Kettering that week and turned up thinking, "Right, we're not going to get dicked here, we're going to do these," and, to be fair, they did,' says Diuk.

The visitors scored early. Midgley was thrilled to score his first goal under Gascoigne, and re-enacted Gazza's famous dentist-chair celebration in tribute. But that was one of the few decent moments for a Kettering side built up as potential giantkillers by a media on Gazzawatch. The players had been told that *Match of the Day* planned to put them on first if they won. As it turned out, they were the last game shown that night, at past midnight, with little more than a few close-ups of Gascoigne and the goals.

Gascoigne's team-talk ahead of the game had been basic, stressing over and over that he didn't want to lose to Graham Westley, the Stevenage manager. 'Nobody comes to our house and beats us,' he told the players. It was a similar story at half-time, with Gascoigne again insisting, 'Don't let this man come into our house and beat us.'

'The Stevenage manager had wound Gazza up before the game and Gazza really didn't want us to get beaten by them,' claimed Midgley. 'He said Chris Waddle had rung him up and told him not to let him beat us. The way he said it, there was so much emotion there, I really wanted to do it for him.'

Paterson, a focal point of the united dressing room during the Wilson era, felt that the players had not been protected enough from the media mayhem in the build-up: 'For a lot of the lads this was the biggest game of their career so far and probably the largest crowd they'd ever experienced. That and the occasion possibly had an effect on some of them.'

He also felt their opponents' fitness had told. Gascoigne, who told the media he was 'very hurt, down and upset after that result', agreed. 'It's a massive difference being full-time. They train with each other every day and by doing so things become second nature. My players have to put in a full day at work and then come training or play a midweek match in the evening.'

He seemed to want to absolve the players of any responsibility for the loss, saying, 'Now I need to pick the players, the club and the town back up.' But the players had accepted defeat by a very good Stevenage side that went close to securing a place in the Football League at the end of that season. As for the town at large, the people of

Kettering enjoyed the occasion, but for many of them the day had always been more about the novelty of seeing Gascoigne on the touchline, rather than any overwhelming desire to see a team they rarely watched give Stevenage a beating.

Kettering's next game at Rockingham Road came a week later, the league fixture against Stalybridge Celtic, and the attendance figure fell by 3,000 to under 1,500. That seemed to catch Ladak and Gascoigne by surprise. When the figure dropped to just 1,132 for Gascoigne's fourth home match as manager a couple of weeks later, against Gainsborough in the FA Trophy, it was obvious the people of Kettering were not maintaining their interest in quite the way the consortium had expected.

To understand why, it is important to consider the nature of the town itself, its region and the people who live there. Although by 2005 its population had grown to just over 50,000, at the turn of the century it was a small market town with a population barely into five figures. The increase that followed was initially inspired by the massive surge in footwear manufacturing in Northamptonshire. The county town of Northampton was the fulcrum for the industry, but sizeable factories serving the likes of Dolcis, Freeman, Hardy and Willis, Frank Wright and Timpsons were also established in Kettering, assimilating workers from both north and south of the town.

After the industry had been decimated by foreign competition, the government designated the town one of its key areas for growth as part of its Milton Keynes and South Midlands Development Plan. This targeted up to 80,000 new homes in the North Northamptonshire sector covering Kettering and nearby Corby.

To help attract and keep the workers needed to man the shoe factories, rows of terraced houses had been built.

Football was already well established and most of the new arrivals brought their allegiances with them and passed them down the generations. Leicester is just 25 miles to the north and its football club, Leicester City, sells plenty of season-tickets in the Kettering area, while Northampton Town retains a loyal band of supporters from families who moved a few miles down the road to help develop the shoe industry.

A sizeable Scottish community was also attracted to the area, partly as a result of the work available in the footwear industry but also because of tens of thousands of jobs in the steel industry. Again, these people brought their allegiances with them, largely to Celtic and Rangers, and handed them on to younger generations. There are big supporters clubs for both Glasgow giants in the area.

The latest wave of migration has seen supporters of clubs up and down the country settle in Kettering without switching their allegiance. Ask people in the town if they support the Poppies, and many will reply, 'Yes, and Manchester United,' (or any other Premier League or Football League club). But the majority still give their first loyalty to the team they normally watch only on television, something Ladak tried to address in his takeover speech when he urged, 'If you support the likes of Manchester United, Chelsea and Liverpool, but aren't at Old Trafford, Stamford Bridge or Anfield on a Saturday afternoon, come along and support your local team.'

Football fans are stubbornly loyal and it can take generations to break down that which passes from father to son. Ladak's hope is that people who can't get to see their Premier League team play live will find heading along to Rockingham Road, or wherever Kettering play their football in the future, a worthy alternative. However, as for so many clubs at this level, competing with the enormous number of

Premier League games shown on TV each week is daunting. A whole generation of fans are growing up with little experience of live games.

Gascoigne was one of a handful of footballers who transcended all boundaries. You didn't have to be a Newcastle, Spurs or Glasgow Rangers fan to appreciate him: his sporting fame was built more on what he did for the national side than for any one club. Added to that, by the time he took over at Kettering, many people related to him more as a 'celebrity' than as a footballer. These people were happy to pop along to gawp at a man who was rarely out of the news for his off-field escapades, but once they'd seen him in the flesh they lost interest in the football. They were not going to be dragged from their sofas to watch what was still a bunch of non-Leaguers in a very cold November month.

It wasn't only among spectators that interest fizzled out. The media had also had its fill. Many of the journalists who had reported on Gascoigne's appointment and first couple of games now turned their attention back to Sir Alex Ferguson, Jose Mourinho and Arsene Wenger. They would come flocking back for one final hurrah, but only when Gascoigne's sacking would provide them with yet more car-crash copy. Many were, of course, proved right for having predicted the inevitable outcome a few weeks earlier.

Although Gascoigne would rant against the national press in particular, he did not enjoy the way in which interest in him as a football manager fell away. At the end of October, journalists had been elbowing each other to get their microphone under his nose. A few weeks later, I was the only one who turned up for the Thursday media get-together to discuss the upcoming Saturday fixture against Stalybridge Celtic.

After arriving at 2.50pm for the agreed 3pm meet time, I sat in the sponsors' lounge on my own for two-and-a-half hours before Gascoigne showed at 5.20pm. There was no apology, although I was later told the 'unavoidable delay' had actually been him going off for a near-40-mile bike ride. At this stage of his life, Gascoigne was as addicted to physical activity as he had been to alcohol, prescription drugs and cigarettes. Hunter Davies, writing Gascoigne's 'fly-on-the-wall' book *Being Gazza*, was quoted in a national newspaper as saying, 'He's not anorexic, but now has this obsessive compulsive disorder for keeping fit. He's virtually knocking on the door of his gym each morning.'

Billingham, who had popped his head around the door of the sponsors' lounge to assure me a couple of times that Gascoigne was on his way, was, as always, at Gascoigne's side during the interview. We spoke for a few minutes about the game just gone and the game to come but he had little to say.

The interview was hard work until I raised the matter of England's friendly international match with Argentina, scheduled for Geneva on the coming Saturday. Then he was happy to give his opinion on the options open to manager Sven-Goran Eriksson and why he felt the Swede could win the World Cup for England the following year. 'I think this is another chance for Sven to experiment with his team,' he told me. 'And if he does experiment with his team and it goes to the worst don't have a go at him. He's trying to get the right formation and the right way to play.'

The previous day's *Evening Telegraph* had carried a two-page spread I had written with Gascoigne in which he again spelled out his plans for the club. As they went to leave, Billingham thanked me for the article. Gascoigne added nothing, but said to Billingham as they walked away, 'Just one – where are they all?'

Some around the club had their problems with Billingham, who they normally had to go through to speak to Gascoigne. Although we'd exchanged a few words over the Tesco story and I didn't like the way he implied I'd broken a confidence, I generally found him a decent guy. He had seen his opportunity and was trying to take it, and who could blame him for that? He wasn't doing anything different to a whole lot of other people at that time.

I was also the only journalist to turn up for the same event the following week, a few days after a disappointing 2–2 draw at lowly Hednesford United and a couple of days ahead of the trip to another struggling side, Vauxhall Motors. I was directed to the boardroom, where a group of students from a media studies course at Northampton University were waiting to greet Gascoigne. They had been bussed in to ask him questions he had been asked a million times before, and they helped fill up the room nicely.

This time, Gascoigne was only a few minutes late. Although Billingham told me to go first, the students did not want to sit there listening to us discussing groin strains, fitness tests and defensive lapses. They wanted to know about his goal at Euro '96 or who should be in the current England team or his worst injury. They were soon jumping in with questions that Gascoigne could parrot answers to without engaging his brain.

I tried to steer the conversation back to current affairs, but it was a lost cause. I enjoyed watching the way he handled the students that afternoon, giving them over half-an-hour of his time and answering their questions in a warm and friendly way. There was no hint of arrogance. He was not asked anything that he had not been asked a thousand times before, and he was happy to sit and chat about the good old days. He was smiling and relaxed.

The students weren't the only ones to go home with good

memories. I drove away from the ground feeling as if I'd gained an insight into the real Paul Gascoigne. Was this the man he was before drink and drugs, and all his other problems, had taken their toll? I'd like to think so. Unfortunately, it was the last time I saw him during his time at Kettering when my primary emotion was not one of concern.

8

RETURN TO THE DENTIST'S CHAIR

WITH A HEALTHY following of away supporters making the short trip from Hertfordshire, the gate for Kettering's FA Cup clash with Stevenage on 5 November was 4,548, the biggest for 11 years, five times the average attendance prior to Gascoigne's arrival and double that which had watched his first match against Droylsden a week previously. Hundreds more were locked out as the turnstiles were closed for safety reasons. Those with a head for heights and desperate not to miss out on the big day climbed on to the rooftops of neighbouring houses to secure their view.

The game against Droylsden had ended in a 1–0 victory. Those three points took Poppies to fourth in the table and the talk was of an unstoppable push for promotion. Fans who had seen their team become the poor relations of their own little corner of Northamptonshire, as Rushden & Diamonds went from nowhere to the Football League without pausing for breath, were suddenly remembering how much potential their club had. Supporters were being quoted by national newspapers. Others were taking to the airwaves on Radio 5 Live and talkSPORT.

One fan who was quoted told *The Observer* that Kettering had been one of the biggest non-League clubs a decade previously, attracting four or five thousand per game. Attendances had fallen off massively since then, but he was sure Gascoigne could immediately double the number of people coming through the turnstiles. It certainly started off that way. But that had been just the sort of talk that had helped persuade Mallinger to buy into the club in 1993, and he had quickly found out for himself that such crowds only came along once in a blue moon. 'Kettering could get four or five thousand,' said Derek Waugh, the deputy sports editor of the *Evening Telegraph,* who had lived in the town for 33 years and covered the club for the paper before Jon Dunham. 'But only on very rare occasions. Peter Mallinger had quickly found out the reality was nothing like four or five thousand a game.'

The big question wasn't whether Gascoigne could bring more people in through the turnstiles. Any fool knew that was going to happen, at least until the novelty wore off. What many people were asking, even as Gascoigne took his place in the dug-out for his first game, was whether he, firstly, had what it took to be a manager at this level and, secondly, whether he'd be hanging around long enough to show he had. Although Gascoigne had lost his rag with the bookmaker offering odds that he'd be gone by Christmas, there were those who believed he was little more than a marketing tool to raise the club's profile and doubted he'd be around too long once the initial surge of enthusiasm had been tempered by the realities of life at this level.

Dave Pace was manager of a Droylsden side that a few days previously had been preparing for just another game. He spoke for many when he said after Gazza's grand opening spectacular: 'All credit to Paul, but the question is when he starts losing three or four will he be sticking around?'

Pace had been wound up by one particular journalist who

he felt was patronising him and his club, trying to paint a picture in which Droylsden were little more than insignificant fall guys for the opposition's celebrity manager: 'I was annoyed by her questions and felt she was being sarcastic towards me. I told her to meet me at the end of the season and we'd see who finished higher. It was us.'

Pace had been warmly greeted by Gascoigne ahead of the game. He got a hug and a kiss. 'All the best, and let's hope it's a good game,' Gascoigne told him.

'He was friendly and warm and didn't look down on us at all,' recalls Pace. 'There were loads of press there and the cameras were right on him all through the game.

'I had a couple of strikers out and they beat us fair and square. Imraan Ladak did his job in getting Gascoigne in because he doubled the crowd. Gascoigne did his job by beating us and giving himself a great start.'

Pace was told after the game that Gascoigne had been drinking, but struggled to believe it. He felt rumour and gossip followed Gascoigne wherever he went, and who was to know the truth? But Gascoigne then walked into the visitors' dressing room. Still wearing his suit, he went around the room shaking hands with the players as they stripped off their kit. He then wandered into the showers to shake hands and talk to a bunch of naked players. 'He just got in the shower with the lads, shaking their hands and wishing them well,' said Pace. 'They had no clothes on and he had his suit, which got soaked. It was strange.

'I had been told he was seen having a drink and I thought that was ludicrous. I thought surely not, but when he was in our dressing room it did look to me as if he'd had a few.'

The win over Droylsden made it six games without conceding a goal. Pace had questioned whether Gascoigne would still be around if the going got tough but few thought such an issue would arise. It was beyond comprehension in those euphoric early days that they would lose many more times over the remaining six months of the season.

But the cynics pointed out that Gascoigne had missed the team gathering the day before the game because of a 'prior engagement' for which no further explanation was offered. Was that a sign of things to come? They also pointed out that, against Droylsden, it was obvious that Davis was the one running affairs from the touchline in his trademark low-key manner, while Gascoigne's involvement seemed to be restricted to a bit of arm-waving and the odd rant at the referee.

The players had only met Gascoigne for the first time an hour before kick-off and had been shocked at how nervous he had appeared. Brett Solkhon, a former Arsenal trainee who had been at Rushden & Diamonds for three-and-a-half years before making the switch to Rockingham Road, combined playing with studying for a sports science degree at Loughborough University.

Having injured his knee a couple of weeks before the takeover, he spent more time with Gascoigne than many of his teammates, sharing regular sessions in the physio room as Gascoigne received treatment on his neck. 'In the changing room on matchdays, Paul would always get very emotional,' he said. 'There were a few times when he was reduced to tears before the game. He'd say things to us like, "You're my boys, we're Kettering Town." Looking back, it was all a little bit cringeworthy. He was so passionate about it.'

Many in the crowd that day could not have cared less how many tears Gascoigne shed in the dressing room. It was enough to have him on their side, bringing a little sunshine to a club that had spent too long in the shade. But it was Davis who the players were taking their direction from, even though some reporters tried to credit Gascoigne with a 'tactical masterstroke' by sending Moore off the bench to net the winning goal. The less exciting truth is that Moore, returning from suspension, only saw action when the young defender Stephan Morley was injured.

By the time of the next game, the FA Cup clash with Stevenage, Wilson had left the club and Gascoigne and Davis were busy imposing their own values on the players. They spent two training sessions that week trying to get the message across on the different way they wanted the team to play.

Although the players were keen to prove what they could do, all the changes being promised by the new regime began to erode the stability of the Wilson era. While some earning a modest wage stacking boxes or delivering letters saw the talk of taking the club full-time as a great opportunity, nobody in those early days knew where they stood. They read the newspaper stories linking all sorts of players to the club and were well aware that Gascoigne could have his pick of footballing talent.

On the other hand, Gazza's name alone was enough to ensure that scouts from the Football League, and perhaps beyond, would start paying some attention to a club that had only really been able to get any serious transfer income by flogging players to other clubs in Northamptonshire: one of their favourite sons, Carl Alford, went to Diamonds for a non-League record fee of £85,000, while goalkeeper Adam Sollitt was a £30,000 departure to Northampton Town.

For the Stevenage game, the club produced what it trumpeted as a limited-edition programme. It had a glossy picture of Gascoigne on the pitch holding aloft a Poppies scarf and carried notes from manager and chairman. Gascoigne's notes added few insights, although he did thank Wilson for his services to the club and spoke of how much he had enjoyed his first week working with the players. Ladak promised supporters that he would run the club in their interests and that he was 'committed to winning games and playing entertaining football'.

Gascoigne sent out a side showing three changes. Despite it being an FA Cup match, all the attention was again off the pitch. Dressed in a shirt and tie, and with the home fans frequently chorusing, 'Gazza, Gazza, give us a wave,' more cameras were focused on Gascoigne than on the game. The snappers knew who would sell their pictures and their papers, and Gascoigne was pretty much the only show in town. Not that he minded: 'The photographers were under his feet all game, but he loved it,' recalled Mike Capps. 'He loved the limelight.'

Gascoigne had been in the boardroom ahead of the match drinking white wine, although there were few discernible signs as he patrolled the technical area in front of the dug-outs. But some of the players claimed that Gascoigne had been upset by Stevenage manager Graham Westley before the match and was quite emotional. For much of the game, he stood at the shoulder of Davis. However, he had to be dragged back to the technical area after being chased down the touchline towards the visitors' goal by a fourth official who seemed just as bemused as everybody else by events in front of the stand.

Stevenage were a good team from a division above Kettering, and their players seemed better able to keep their focus. They ran out deserved 3–1 winners with young George Boyd, scorer of their second goal, the destroyer-in-chief. Anthony Elding came off the subs' bench to net the third goal that killed off any hopes of a Kettering revival after Neil Midgley had cancelled out Darryn Stamp's opener.

The visitors deserved their win and, although Gascoigne tried to dismiss the defeat with the line, 'We were never going to win the FA Cup anyway,' the performance was a disappointment. Many of the players were honest enough to admit they had not performed. Some had found the burden of expectation, and the distractions, too much. It was different running out in front of a capacity crowd with the *Match of the Day* cameras zooming in on them, having just had their name read out by Gascoigne. But they knew only too well who everybody had to come to see. 'It was all about Paul,' says Christian Moore. 'I never kidded myself it was about me. It was all about Paul, he was the celebrity.'

It wasn't only Kettering's players who found the day at odds with everything that had gone on before. The small press box at Rockingham Road seats just half-a-dozen journalists and there was nowhere big enough to stage the post-match conference other than the social club. However, this was packed with supporters. Some were, no doubt, hoping that Gascoigne would pay them a visit in the same way he had after the previous match, when he had been handed a bottle of Newcastle Brown: he put his thumb over the top of the bottle, gave it a good shake and sprayed beer over fans who lapped up their moment in the Gascoigne spotlight. Another chant of 'Gazza, Gazza, Gazza' rang out.

The reporters gathered on the pitch at the end of the tunnel and, after the TV interviews had been conducted outside the dressing rooms, Billingham brought Gascoigne out to face another barrage of questions. Again, far more were about everything other than the game itself, but Gascoigne indulged in mainly 'football-speak' and shrugged off the defeat with the cliché about concentrating on the league. No doubt as a result of his years being pursued by journalists in this country and abroad, he had developed the ability to reply to a question with an answer that bore no correlation to what he had been asked.

Although he was polite, he was clearly anxious to be back within the confines of the club. He walked back down the tunnel to find a Stevenage player waiting for him, holding a copy of Gascoigne's confessional book, *My Story*, which he politely asked 'Mr Gascoigne' to autograph.

Although Gascoigne had tried to insist that all that had mattered on that hectic day had been 'my players', there was no getting away from the fact that everything had again been largely about him. Indeed, his own players acknowledged that with a goal celebration that mimicked Gascoigne's infamous 'dentist's chair' effort nine years earlier after he scored against Scotland in Euro '96.

Ahead of that tournament, Gascoigne, who had been crowned Scottish Player of the Year a month earlier, as he helped Glasgow Rangers to an eighth successive title, had been part of an England squad bonding trip to Hong Kong. To celebrate his 29th birthday, Gascoigne and a clutch of players headed to a nightclub which featured a 'dentist's chair' in which you sat, mouth open, to have alcohol poured straight from the bottle down your throat.

Photographs of players with ripped shirts clutching bottles of drink made their way to the national press in England, and the papers had a field day. Hysteria was whipped up further when it was revealed that on the Cathay Pacific flight home drunken players had caused £5,000 worth of damage to two widescreen television screens. Again the finger of blame was pointed at Gascoigne. The issue caused the Football Association severe embarrassment and was debated by Members of Parliament, some of whom called for both Gascoigne and Terry Venables, the England manager, to be sacked.

However, all was forgiven, if not forgotten, when Gascoigne scored his stunning goal against Scotland at Wembley a short while later, lifting the ball over the hapless Colin Hendry with his left foot before firing home past Andy Goram with his right to help England to a famous victory over the old enemy. Gascoigne celebrated by rushing to the side of the Scotland goal and throwing himself flat out on his back, mouth open and arms outstretched. Teddy Sheringham picked up a conveniently placed bottle and jetted water down his throat. It was a cheeky snipe back at the critics, but, with the country now firmly behind their talisman and their team, even the nationals' news editors found it impossible not to smile.

It was an image that had stuck in the memory of the players now under Gascoigne at Rockingham Road. So when Midgley fired the goal against Stevenage, they acted out their own version. 'All the boys spoke about it during the training session on the Thursday before the game and asked each other what we should do if we scored a goal,' said Solkhon. 'That celebration was the first thing that everybody came up with.

'When Midge scored, all the boys ran over to where myself and Junior McDougald were waiting with water bottles. We never told Gazza about it before [but] he likes a laugh and a joke.'

A star-struck Midgley was horrified to find himself exchanging words with Gascoigne early in the game after the manager had screamed at him to hold the ball up: 'The ball didn't come down for ages and I had this big centre-half right behind me and he shouted at me, "Midge, come on, you've got to get hold of the ball." I'm thinking, "I really am trying but the ball isn't coming to me." He shouted at me two or three times and I ended up biting back, saying, "I am fucking trying." Then the ball bounced in the area, I've taken a touch onto my left foot, my weakest foot, and I've scuffed a shot. It's gone through a few legs and I'm lying on the floor thinking, "Just go in." It did and I ran to the bench for the celebration.'

Gascoigne loved it. He looked up to ex-England and Newcastle winger Chris Waddle, sitting in the stands, and pointed at his players as if to say, 'Look what the lads are doing for me.' He was flattered that this modest group of part-timers were re-enacting one of his most iconic moments.

The Stevenage fans had plenty to say as their team took Gascoigne's apart. 'Gazza out, Gazza out' was the cry when they went ahead. That became, 'Gazza, Gazza, what's the score?' after their second goal. When the third went in, around 1,000 visiting fans sang, 'Cry in a minute, he's going to cry in a minute.'

Although some around the club had spoken of their disappointment at the players failing to perform, there was so much else to look forward to that they put aside their disappointment. The talk of a new ground, new reserve team, new signings and the playing squad going full-time saw to that. The FA Cup could wait for another year, Gascoigne and Ladak had already made it clear that getting into the Football League was the priority. They were convincing in their promises and, after 133 years of exclusively non-League football, the dream seemed closer to becoming reality than it had ever been.

9

WHO WANTS A LAMBORGHINI?

TO SOME, the most incredible aspect of Gascoigne's only spell as a football manager was the speed at which it all unravelled. The cynics got it right with their predictions of a tear-stained finale, but Kettering only lost their first league game under Gascoigne on 22 November. By 5 December, he was gone.

Gascoigne's mood swings were a talking point among people at the club within a fortnight of his arrival. Even he was forced to admit his behaviour was unacceptable three days after the defeat by Stevenage.

Alfreton Town on a wet and windy Tuesday night was just the sort of fixture that was thrown at Gascoigne and Davis when these big names from the upper echelons of the sport walked through the door at Rockingham Road. 'It grates with me a bit when the suggestion is we wouldn't fancy a wet Tuesday night at a northern club,' complained Davis. 'Both Paul and I have faced challenges throughout our playing careers and we are looking forward to another one.'

They headed for the small town off junction 28 of the M1

between Nottingham and Sheffield, determined to put the defeat by Stevenage behind them.

Davis was also hoping that the intense media spotlight would let up. 'There will always be media interest when the gaffer is involved. Wherever he goes, the press will follow. But, hopefully, now it will ease off a little and we can concentrate on the football.' Davis admitted he had been concerned that all the fuss had affected the players, adding, 'Now that will hopefully not be an issue and we can get on with the important issue of winning football matches.'

Unfortunately, things were not to be that simple. Alfreton's biggest gate of the season had been 388, and they had averaged under 300. However, they were hoping for a four-figure turnout, perhaps as many as 2,000, because of the star turn. They were set to get it, with several hundred people having paid their £8 to enter the Impact Arena before 7pm. But then the weather, and the referee, intervened to leave Gascoigne red-faced and angry. The match was called off 35 minutes before kick-off with the pitch waterlogged. A bad-tempered Gascoigne accused the host club of engineering the postponement to cover up an injury crisis.

Gascoigne had been out on the muddy pitch with the officials during their 20-minute inspection. It had been raining for much of the day, and with parts of the pitch covered in puddles, referee Gary Mellor felt he had no choice, despite the crowd swarming through the turnstiles. 'Fans have come down here wanting to watch Paul's team, but it would have been a farce,' he said. 'Players' safety has to come into it.'

Gascoigne threw his arms up in despair. He told the referee it was 'bollocks'. He followed the officials off the pitch, ignoring the autograph hunters lining the tunnel area, and harangued them in their dressing room. As always, his language was liberally sprinkled with swear words. He later returned to apologise to Mellor. But an hour after the decision he was shaking as he huddled around the dressing-room door, with Billingham and Ladak doing their best to calm him.

When asked what had upset him so much, Gascoigne said, 'I've had 29 operations – broken noses, broken arms, broken cheekbones – and it's always been when the pitch has been dry. The referee said one side of the pitch was OK, the other wasn't. I said it could be a game of two halves. We could have the advantage one half and them the other.'

It appears Gascoigne's temper had been fuelled by drinking wine on the coach on the way to the game. That was the day when many of the players say it became obvious he had a drink problem. Although he tried to keep a bottle of wine hidden on the coach, he was unsteady on his feet by the time he came to get off and fell down the steps.

'He literally fell off the bus,' says Brett Solkhon. 'With all the press that had started following us around, I was amazed there wasn't a reporter there to see it. He stormed onto the pitch and accused the home team of waterlogging it on purpose, saying they'd got the hoses out and that they were frightened to play us. This all happened with the Sky Sports News cameras there and it was a lot for us to take in. There were cameras everywhere and none of us were used to that.'

'That was the point when I thought, "He doesn't know what he's doing, he's not in control of his body,"' recalls Andy Hall. 'As a player, you'd see someone stumbling about before a game and think, "This isn't right," but you've just got to get on with it. I couldn't influence what he did, I could only do what I could do. I didn't feel any embarrassment because it wasn't me doing it. I felt sorry for him.'

A few hours earlier, Jim Wykes had been resting upstairs in his pub, The Beeswing, when the phone rang. 'Gazza wants pasta and rice, enough for 15 people, by the time the bus leaves for the game tonight,' he was told. 'It wasn't Gazza would *like*, it was Gazza *wants*,' says Wykes. 'We don't keep pasta like that, so we raced to the Bookers cash-and-carry, got the big pots on, cooked the pasta, rice and a sauce and put it in our catering trays. I took them to the ground, where everybody was sitting on the bus with the engine ticking over. "Who do I give the bill to?" I asked the driver.'

He was told to send it to the club. He got the same phone call the following week and again raced the food to the waiting bus. He submitted two invoices to the club for £80 each. They were never paid. 'I didn't chase them up,' he confesses. 'The joy of doing it for Gazza!'

*   *   *

Although Kettering got all the media coverage at Alfreton, for the home club the night had been a financial disaster. They had to refund the admission money to supporters as they trooped back out through the turnstiles, and probably made a loss. A number of quick-witted young fans took the £8 and then climbed back into the ground over a wall behind one of the goals. They then passed through the turnstiles again, collecting another £8 on the way.

Gascoigne's mood was not helped by the knowledge that he now had only one training session that week. He again spoke about the need to go full-time, but the difference in ability between what he had been used to as a player himself and what he was faced with at Kettering was an issue even he acknowledged: 'I have got to learn to be patient and realise the standard of the players I am working with.'

According to the players, Gascoigne's nerves always came to the fore on match days. 'He was this flamboyant character as a player, but all his problems meant he had gone from that person to this underweight bloke in a suit that was too big for him,' said Diuk. 'He was just really nervous. I imagine he had a lot of pressure on him with the whole country wanting to know how he'd get on.'

'He was never drunk or drinking at training, it was only on match days,' recalls Solkhon. 'He was just overexcited, the pressure got to him. You could see how easily persuaded he was. It started happening every week, home and away.'

After the postponement at Alfreton, Ladak had spoken of the 'very interesting' team selection that Gascoigne had come up with. All was revealed when the manager named his side for the home game against Stalybridge. To the players, it was a sign of things to come: Liam Nicell was dropped to the bench as Gascoigne brought in the raw 17-year-old Stephan Morley at left-back, and popular central midfield duo Jamie Paterson and Hugh McAuley kept Nicell company in the dug-out. Gascoigne paired centre-half David Theobald and winger Andy Hall in the engine room.

But the game went well and Gascoigne's selections and tactics were justified. They produced an outstanding performance that provided a tantalising glimpse of quite how good life could have been under Gascoigne if all the other issues had not got in the way. James Gould scored a 20-yard opener that Gascoigne himself would have been proud of. Theobald, thrilled to have been handed the No. 8 shirt, netted his first goal for the club with a thumping right-foot volley. The excellent Gould set up the recalled Ollie Burgess for a headed third before firing in a fierce shot from the edge of the box that deflected in off Christian Moore.

The manager was on a high and enthused about the 'unbelievable team spirit' in the dressing room. But, despite enjoying the win and the praise, the players had been disturbed when Gascoigne strayed a couple of yards on to the pitch in the first half. Some had also noticed him dashing backwards and forwards between the stand and the dug-out, and then down the tunnel. 'I don't think he knew where he was,' said one.

One person who tried hard to keep an eye on a hyperactive Gascoigne during that game was Stalybridge boss John Reed. He had been greeted on arrival at Rockingham Road with a kiss on the cheek by Gascoigne. Then, as both teams warmed up before kick-off, the Kettering manager sneaked up behind him to give him another one.

There was more. Reed watched open mouthed as Gascoigne's team tore his side apart and, when the home side's third goal went in, Gazza sprinted down from the stand to plant another kiss on Reed's cheek. The crowd behind them erupted. They teased Reed mercilessly as he tried to focus on the game while keeping an eye out for any further movement towards him from Gascoigne: 'We're losing 3–1 and all I'm thinking is I've been kissed three times by Gazza. We ended up losing 4–1 and I had a terrific day. Him on the touchline definitely took the edge off some of my lads, they were in awe of him. He had me laughing so much, and I don't do that when my team's losing.'

With so much happening around them, Reed was not surprised that his players had been a little star-struck. But he was disappointed with their work-rate and, on their return to the dressing room, ordered them to sit down. 'I start hammering them and then suddenly the door opens. There's no knock. It's Gazza, he's carrying a pint glass that's over half full of whisky and he walks up and gives to me.'

'Knock that back, bonnie lad,' Gascoigne told Reed as the players fell about laughing.

As Reed started drinking, Gascoigne walked around the dressing room to shake hands with all the players. Semi-dressed and naked footballers scrambled to lay their hands on anything they could find to get Gascoigne to sign. He did the rounds, waved goodbye and departed.

Reed, no longer capable of continuing his rollicking, told his players to shower and change: 'Then he [Gascoigne] came back in and walked around shaking hands again. Half the lads were in the shower but he just walked in and talked to them.'

Gascoigne's clothing was soaked on his return to his own team's dressing room but he didn't care: 'Their manager said that was the best football he'd seen at that level in his whole career,' he told his players.

'He seemed quite flattered by that,' observed Diuk.

Next up was the Monday-night game against Hednesford Town, who were struggling near the foot of the table and had been thumped 6–2 by Worcester City on the day Kettering crushed Stalybridge. Even the club's own website report had slammed their team's 'shambolic defending'.

This game was the first of three on the trot against sides at the wrong end of the table, and confidence was high among supporters that their team would claim nine points to boost their title credentials. Although Gascoigne named the same starting line-up as for the previous match, that was pretty much all the games had in common.

On a bitterly cold night in Staffordshire, Gascoigne was sitting in the stand drinking from a coffee cup when the game kicked off. His side went a goal behind after 47 seconds and he was straight out of his seat and patrolling the touchline, wearing only an open-neck shirt and flimsy jacket. As he shivered in temperatures close to zero, his side went a further goal behind. Gascoigne again wandered on to the pitch before being shepherded back by the fourth official, who spent much of the rest of the game keeping a close eye on him.

'We were laughing and joking ahead of that game, I think maybe we had got a bit arrogant,' said Diuk. 'We were 2–0 down after 20 minutes playing a system where the full-backs were basically starting on the halfway line. I remember standing on the halfway line and our right midfielder, Ollie Burgess, a great player, saying to me, "If you're there, where do I go?" He couldn't go any further forward because he was going to be offside. I told him, "Don't ask me, I don't know."'

It was the same on the other flank, where young Morley made a hesitant start.

Prior to kick-off, Gascoigne had again done his good deed by being photographed on the pitch with a couple of pretty young models who were promoting Hednesford's new away shirt. It had nothing to do with him but, as so often, when asked to do a favour, he obliged. Mike Capps had been approached by one of the home directors to take the picture, and he knocked on the dressing-room door to ask Gascoigne if he would pose with the girls. 'He was great about things like that,' said Capps. 'He didn't often say no.'

But the match that followed didn't go anything like as smoothly. Like a number of his teammates, Moore was troubled by the changes forced on them. He felt the small amount of time they'd had at training to work on new systems and formations could only lead to confusion. Even when they were 2–0 down and being embarrassed, Davis insisted the back four continue passing the ball to each other. As often as not, they did just that until the ball was given away.

Moore scored shortly before half-time to finally give Kettering something to cheer and a point was secured when Gould fired home another stunning left-footer in the second half. Despite Gascoigne insisting afterwards, 'we are starting to play football the way I like it played,' the draw was more a result of a long-held fighting spirit than of any great tactical masterplan.

'I don't know what they'd watched before they came to the club but Conference North is a different world, no matter how good a player you've been at the highest level,' said Moore. 'The back four were told they had to keep the ball and it looked pretty, but from where I was up front it was crap. We never went forward. All the ball did was go across the back four. Everyone we played just sat off and watched us do it.

'Derek Brown and Craig McIlwain thought they were Franz Beckenbauer and were loving it, keeping the ball for half the game. But the ball never came forward, it just ended up going nowhere.

'The lads couldn't do anything about it, it was the way they wanted you to play. It might look lovely on a Premiership ground but when you're playing away in Conference North on a Monday night it doesn't work. I knew a lot of lads in non-League and they sat off and let us have the ball because we weren't hurting them. They were more bothered by trying to find out what Gazza was like.'

However, Davis was having none of that, insisting, 'We want them to play and they can play. We believe they are good enough to play good football and win matches with attacking football.'

Gascoigne agreed. 'We don't look like a non-League team. We look like a team that's bringing the ball down, playing good football and creating chances.'

After the game, Gascoigne had wandered off on his own to an empty room high up in the main stand away from the dressing room. He stood there shivering. During the match, a padded coat had been retrieved from the dug-out for him, but this had been stripped off. He smoked cigarette after cigarette. After refusing to talk to the two journalists waiting to interview him, he eventually agreed to speak to us one at a time.

Gascoigne's behaviour that day had further troubled some of his players. On the coach on the way to the game, the players whispered among themselves about the smell of alcohol. One by one, a few of them made excuses to wander to the front of the coach, where they saw a half-empty bottle of wine down the side of Gascoigne's seat.

Moore claimed that Gascoigne had little idea what had happened on the pitch that evening. 'After going 2–0 down, we chased the game and pulled it back to 2–1. He didn't realise we had scored. When we equalised, he thought the score was 2–1 to them. He really struggled to cope with matches.'

To his dismay, Capps had also picked up how things went downhill once the game was underway. Having taken pictures of a composed Gascoigne with the models less than an hour earlier, Capps was surprised at what he saw when he targeted his lens on the manager early into the game: 'He was so nervous, he was shaking. He was getting upset over nothing. He wasn't the same man.'

After the players had boarded the coach for the return trip, Gascoigne stood up and started waving a set of keys around flamboyantly. He said he had an announcement to make. From now on, each man of the match would get a Lamborghini for a week. But if there was a Lamborghini, nobody got to drive it, and it was never mentioned again.

The point from that game kept Kettering fifth in the table. Gascoigne accepted it was two points dropped but knew victories at bottom club Vauxhall Motors and another club in the relegation scrap, Redditch United, over the next week would make the messy first half at Hednesford a distant memory. However, with some players becoming increasingly distracted by talks over new contracts and turning full-time, Kettering could only draw 1–1 against a Vauxhall Motors side who had Thomas Rooney, cousin of Wayne, sent off for two poor fouls in the first 22 minutes.

They then turned in a wretched performance to lose 2–1 to Redditch. Rather than the keenly anticipated nine points, their trips to three of the bottom four had yielded just two.

By the time the Redditch game was over, there was open dissent within the squad.

Gascoigne's response to the draw at Vauxhall Motors, who had come close to winning the game in the final minutes, was to make decisions that baffled players and supporters alike. The team's captain, Derek Brown, missed the Tuesday-night trip to Redditch through injury, but, instead of switching David Theobald from his unaccustomed role in midfield, Gascoigne paired regular full-back Diuk with McIlwain in the centre of defence. Two days before the match, he had sent Diuk a text message asking him whether he wanted to play centre-half.

Diuk had received Gascoigne's text during his daughter's christening. Having picked up a knock at Vauxhall Motors the day before, he wasn't even sure he'd be fit for Redditch and was enjoying a couple of drinks. 'He texted to ask if I was going to be fit for Tuesday because he wanted to play me centre-half,' said Diuk. 'I was, like, what's going on here, I hadn't played centre-half all season. But I said, yeah, I'd be fit and he texted back to say that's great because he wanted Andy Hall in centre midfield. Andy was the quickest lad at the club and had been destroying teams on the wing, yet now he was in centre midfield with a centre-half alongside him.

'Then before the game, the gaffer pulled me to one side and said you can either play centre-half or centre midfield. I remember thinking to myself, "If I play centre midfield then my good mate Jamie Paterson is going to stay on the bench, but if I play centre-half then Patto might get back in the side," and he was a very good player. I said I'd play centre-half but he still put David Theobald in midfield. He was a good player but he'll tell you himself he was a centre-half.'

Elsewhere along the back four, Morley was given a torrid time by David Hollis, who had a big hand in both goals. But the entire back four were hesitant and uncertain. It seemed

Redditch had done their homework, sitting deep when the Poppies had the ball in their own half and pressing relentlessly whenever the ball got moved forward. With little space to play in, Gascoigne's side regularly surrendered possession and were hit by a couple of sucker punches. 'Teams all of a sudden realised this was how we played and we had no plan B,' says Diuk. 'We weren't allowed a plan B.'

Diuk found himself up against a huge striker who won everything in the air and fed on the chaos that Hollis caused down the Poppies' left flank.

'You're willing to play anywhere for your manager,' says Hall. 'I gave it 110 per cent but it wasn't my best position.' Some of the more senior players also questioned the decision. Hall explains Gascoigne's reasoning: 'He said to me, "You're one of my best players on the ball so I want you on the ball as much as possible in the right area, which is the centre." He said, "I need you in a position where you can influence the game," whereas out wide he didn't feel I could do that as much. Being a wide man or full-back my whole career, it's pretty easy to cope with being moved up and down the field but when you go inside it's different. You've got to be cleverer on the ball, you've got more responsibility. If you haven't played there much and don't know the position, you're going to be affected by it.'

Gascoigne admitted after the game that words had been said in the dressing room, while Gould, who had been one of the better players during Gascoigne's reign, made the obvious point, 'our midfield were not really in it.'

The watching Jon Dunham describes Kettering's performance as absolutely awful, and witnessed a shaken Gascoigne leave the ground: 'A lot of the fans from Redditch stayed behind to get his autograph and he just ran through them all. He didn't sign one, and that was one thing he had done until then. He just got on the coach and left. It didn't feel right.'

Although Gascoigne again said he was proud of his

players, they had lost much of the self-belief and unity which had underpinned their form under Wilson.

'We started on a downward spiral and the football we were playing was awful. We were shipping goals left, right and centre and pointing the finger at each other, and we'd never done that before,' recalled Diuk. 'The season was changing from we're going to win this league to starting to look down at the bottom of the table and thinking, "If we're not careful we're going to end up there."'

Most of the players had idolised Gascoigne a decade earlier and could not believe the way things were going. 'People were being played out of position and maybe the drinking played a part in that,' Solkhon reflects. 'Paul Davis was taking all the training and towards the end he was doing the team talks as well. Sometimes he found it hard to put his point across and sometimes he was too quiet. Other times we'd need an answer to a problem we were having on the pitch and he didn't know what to say.'

The dressing room fractured, but not only because of the poor performances and puzzling team selections. Gascoigne and Ladak had raised expectations over money, and all the gossip over full-time contracts or new part-time deals became a distraction. To the players, there seemed to be no proper structure in place to sort out the details. They were given a form to fill in asking them how much money they wanted to give up their day jobs, and several complained that nobody then spoke to them about it.

Some senior players felt the management were not being straight, and two leading players both complained they were given offers only to see them withdrawn. Others felt the manager had no understanding of what a big decision it was for a working man to gamble his family's security by quitting his job for a full-time contract that meant a drop in income and would probably only cover a year or two. One player was told they wanted him to go full-time but, having explained he didn't want to give up his day job, he felt he was never treated the same again.

While the senior players spoke openly of their frustration, others with the club at heart couldn't understand the logic behind Gascoigne's team selections. 'There were changes galore yet for some reason Stephan Morley was the only player who seemed certain of a place,' says Peter Mallinger, who felt that the teenager had not shown the right attitude in the summer when he missed some pre-season training to go on holiday and then skipped another session to see a show.

'With that sort of commitment, you could reason it would not be long before Stephan was back playing park football,' says Mallinger. 'So what was it that Paul Gascoigne saw that made him play Stephan every match when more established players couldn't make the team? It was a mystery to everyone. It wouldn't have been so bad if Stephan had played well, but in the main he was awful. Yet he was always in Paul Gascoigne's next team.'

Some of the senior players also questioned whether Morley was ready for the first team at such a tender age, although they were sympathetic to a young lad who had not yet reached his 18th birthday and was in the firing line. 'Steph was a good player, but he was young and there was a lot of pressure on him,' says Diuk. 'I was feeling the pressure myself, so, for a lad who was only 17 at the time, you could see it. He was going on the pitch looking pressured.'

Although behind-the-scenes issues were contributing to the general sense of disarray, the players felt they could have coped with that if things on the pitch had been different. But Gascoigne's chop-and-change team selections and Davis's insistence on the alien passing game meant they were taking to the pitch questioning themselves. This was their reason for the decline in results. They could have put up with all the baggage that came with Gascoigne if they had been left to get on with the jobs they had done well enough until the end of October. They were not only being denied this, they were being told it was wrong.

'Paul would get frustrated with the players because they couldn't play the way he wanted them to play,' says Solkhon. 'The lads started to question the management and felt it was a bit of a joke. The novelty wore off very quickly. People started to see how it was going and we all knew where it was heading.'

But there were some who couldn't wait to give up their day job and go full-time. One was Andy Hall, who had spent three years in the youth ranks of Coventry City before being released that summer, and he saw Gascoigne's arrival as the chance to make his name. In their first phone conversation, Gascoigne said he had received glowing reports about the blond teenager, who had started as a wing-back but had been used further forward by Wilson. Although they hadn't met yet, Gascoigne told him he was a big part of his plans.

While more senior players waited to discover how Gascoigne saw their future, Hall was handed a two-year full-time contract, the first to get a deal, and he didn't care what anyone else thought: 'For someone like Paul Gascoigne to come in and say you're one of my best players and I want to sign you for a long period, it was an honour for me.'

He was to be paid just over £350 a week, but says that the money didn't have much to do with it: 'I saw it as my opportunity. I wanted to be a professional footballer and you think you can play for a Premiership club. I was thinking the manager might get another club and might take me with him. The other players didn't say anything to me. They could have been bickering at each other about me, saying he's getting this amount, he's getting that amount, but they never said anything to me. If you get your chance, you've got to take it.'

With the players looking at each other in the dressing room and wondering who was, and who wasn't, going to profit from the changes, team spirit began to implode. Whereas players had been happy to sit next to anyone as they got changed, now allegiances started to form.

'We'd gone from a unit to the lads starting to fall out,' says Diuk. 'A few of the lads got promised a lot and it upset the balance. Big players fell out with the gaffer over how he was using them. Before all this, with Kev, you knew where you stood. If you weren't in his plans you were gone, he'd never promise you anything and not deliver. We had people starting to go into cliques, a few here, a few there, whereas it used to be everyone together. You'd sit anywhere and have a laugh with whoever was next to you. Not any more.'

Meanwhile, Ladak found himself receiving a growing list of complaints about Gascoigne's drinking, and he was finding it hard to talk to his increasingly paranoid manager. When the pressure got too much, Gascoigne took to his office and shut the door. On one occasion, Ladak opened the door to find Gascoigne drunk, and told Davis to drive him home.

Managing Gascoigne's decline was consuming time and resources that would have been better spent elsewhere, with many of the players believing not enough attention was being given to their concerns. 'I think they were more worried about what Paul was up to, to be honest,' says Diuk.

It was not the best time to bring in a bunch of new players, but, with Gascoigne having decided that fresh impetus was needed, three new faces were introduced in the space of a week – but they were not the big names that had been talked about at the time of the takeover.

Attacking midfielder Ryan-Zico Black signed on 17 November from Lancaster City and made his debut from the bench two days later at Vauxhall Motors, having disguised a calf injury. His signing was followed by the return to the club of striker Michael McKenzie after an 18-month absence. Newcastle United reserve Kevin Dixon signed a day after playing in Kettering's first reserve game against Stafford Rangers.

'I got a phone call asking if I would be interested in coming down here and, to be honest, the offer was too good to refuse,' he revealed.

With a number of the established players frustrated at their own lack of offers, that statement would do little to help team spirit.

A fourth signing was 21-year-old Jordan Fowler, a tough-tackling midfielder who was a product of the Arsenal academy and had played for the Gunners reserves that autumn. He signed six days before Gascoigne and Davis left the club and played for just 32 minutes of their final game against Barrow.

To further emphasise the divisions in the dressing room, it was announced two days ahead of that game that four players were to be sent to Milton Keynes Dons for daytime training, following a deal struck between Ladak and Dons chairman Pete Winkelman. Ladak enthused, 'To have four players training over 15 hours a week instead of two or three will improve fitness, sharpness and ability.'

The four selected to work with Danny Wilson's squad at Dons were Hall, Dixon, McKenzie and Fowler, but not the newly signed Black, who was still travelling from his Lancaster home and struggling with injury. The rest of the players were simply told to continue doing their day jobs as the move to a fully professional squad dragged on.

The plan was for the quartet to train under Gascoigne and Davis on Tuesday and Thursday evenings, matches permitting, and to spend four mornings a week at Milton Keynes, where Winkelman had set about building a new ground and training facilities after controversially moving the club from their South London home to the National Hockey Centre. The agreement covered the whole of December, with Ladak still hoping to take Kettering full-time early the following year.

Until he was packed off to Dons for daytime training, Hall had only been required to attend the normal evening squad sessions for the first couple of weeks of his full-time contract. He took it on himself to look after his own fitness, and said nobody checked to see what he was up to. He was glad to get the chance to train with Football League players, although that was something Black was hesitant about when he was finally told to join the others in travelling to Milton Keynes. He had yet to force his way into the team and wasn't sure how training with one set of coaches and players would help him prove he deserved his chance with another set 40 miles away.

For many of the players who had been at the club before the takeover, all this activity, much of which they only heard about through gossip, contributed to the discord. Jamie Paterson was one of the most popular players and had been voted the supporters' player of the year the previous season. But after he said he didn't want to go full-time, and voiced his doubts about the direction the club was heading in under Gascoigne, he was told to leave.

Paterson's car-buddy Moore was so angry at the way he was treated when Gascoigne decided he didn't want him around the club anymore that he drove from his Staffordshire home to confront the man who had once been his footballing idol. He decided he had to get away for the sake of his peace of mind, and was promptly placed on the transfer list.

Gascoigne told Jon Dunham when questioned, 'If they don't want to play for Kettering and they want to leave, then fine, they can do that.'

He clearly couldn't see that the pair, highly valued by their teammates and supporters, felt the club had changed so much in just a few weeks that they were no longer playing for the same one.

Others outside the dressing room wondered how the players were coping. 'One thing I learned in my time involved with players is that they are very, very quick to pick up any weaknesses in the manager and exploit them. That's what players do. If it was the case that Gascoigne was flawed, as I'm sure it was, that would have manifested itself to the players,' claims Dave Dunham.

Staff at the Kettering Park Hotel, where Gascoigne normally headed after matches and training, told of his spending more time in the bar from mid-November, where it seemed brandy had replaced white wine as his drink of choice. Workers turning up for the early shift one morning were surprised to find Gascoigne wandering around the kitchen trying to find something to eat.

Ladak was disturbed by reports of Gascoigne's drinking, and raised the issue with Billingham, who he hoped might still have influence over Gascoigne. Indeed, he was so concerned he feared the man he had once worshipped as a footballer 'could end up paying with his life'.

Gascoigne admits he was feeling the strain of being a 'gaffer', especially once results nosedived. Expectations had been so high that a run of three games without a win constituted a crisis, and it hadn't helped that the trio of clubs were struggling at or near the bottom.

Escaping the pressure wasn't easy in a small town like Kettering. He had had to leave Champneys, where he had stayed free of charge, and moved permanently into the Kettering Park Hotel. By now, a couple of national newspaper journalists were digging around for stories about his drinking, and the hotel was an easier place to spy on him than the health farm.

On the *Evening Telegraph* sports desk, we often answered our phones to find journalists from around the world chasing our opinions and any salacious gossip we might like to pass on. One caller, who said he worked for a national tabloid, told Jon Dunham, 'I remember what it was like to work on a local paper and, let's be honest, the pay is pretty poor. If you help us, I'll get you some money.'

There are plenty of people in Kettering, including former directors, fans and players, who felt Gascoigne had only been brought to the club to raise its profile. There was nothing in his recent past to suggest he could make it stick, even if he had convinced himself this was his big opportunity. They felt the club was paying a heavy price for that.

Now, with attendances dipping sharply, Gascoigne having failed to come up with the money he'd agreed to stake, a transfer fee to be paid, the introduction of full-time contracts and a reserve team to fund, Ladak was having to dig deep. He was also throwing money away on Gascoigne's whims, and was troubled by what he was hearing from the dressing room. He no longer trusted his manager to make the right decisions.

Mallinger, at that stage still working as the chairman's right-hand man, says that Ladak experienced some eccentric and expensive behaviour from Gascoigne. 'Typical was the hiring of a Toyota 4x4 for a week. It just stood in the same spot in the car park. He was never sober enough to drive it. It never seemed to occur to him that Imraan had to pay the bill.'

This after the local Mercedes garage had offered both Gascoigne and Davis top-of-the-range sponsored cars. 'Anything they wanted seemed within their grasp,' Mallinger adds.

The demand for anything related to Gascoigne seemed insatiable, and Mallinger has spoken of people turning up at the club's offices trying to track him down to tell their hard-

Above: A relaxed and happy Paul Gascoigne on his appointment as manager.

Below: Gascoigne's appointment generated massive interest in the non-League club. "It was like the second coming," said local councillor Chris Smith-Haynes.

Pictures Mike Capps/www.kappasport.co.uk

Key men: ambitious new chairman Imraan Ladak (*left*) and Gascoigne talked about signing the likes of Mark Bosnich, Teddy Sheringham and Les Ferdinand. Ladak bought the club from Peter Mallinger (*below*), who was disturbed by his first impression of Gascoigne.

Pictures: Mike Capps/www.kappasport.co.uk

Gascoigne's No. 2, Paul Davis (*above*), was an Arsenal legend. He showed the part-time players a video of France beating Brazil in the 1998 World Cup final and told them this was how they were going to play. Former manager Kevin Wilson (*right*) said: "I sat there wishing I wasn't there, feeling like a spare prick at a wedding," after finding himself squeezed out following Gascoigne's appointment.

Pictures: Mike Capps/www.kappasport.co.uk.

Left: Gascoigne enjoyed all the fuss his return to football generated, even if it was at a club that had never played in the Football League. He was spotted in the crowd with an entourage that included his pal Jimmy 'Five Bellies' Gardner (*below*).

Below: His good mate Chris Waddle went along to give Gazza support when he could.
Pictures: Mike Capps/www.kappasport.co.uk.

Left: Ryan-Zico Black (*top left*) was the first signing of the Gazza reign but quickly found himself the centre of a row between chairman and manager. Gazza told him: "When I was playing I thought I was better than Pele, Best, Maradona. I probably wasn't, but I honestly believed I was when I was on the pitch."

Above: Christian Moore (*right*) celebrates a goal in happier times, with Andy Hall. The highly-experienced veteran striker had his differences with Gazza. "He wasn't a bad bloke. He was just a bloke with too many problems who'd been given the wrong job."
Pictures: Mike Capps/ www.kappasport.co.uk

Above: Long-serving Wayne Diuk was promised a testimonial game featuring a host of big names. "I think they thought it was Championship Manager on the computer, they really did. We'll go in there, we'll buy this player and this player and we'll be in the Premier League in a few years."

Right: Promising youngster Andy Hall (*right*) with Ollie Burgess. "They knew we had Gazza and managers were saying things to their players like, 'These are big-time Charlies and we need to get into their faces.'"
Pictures: Mike Capps/ www.kappasport.co.uk

Left: Gascoigne provided plenty of entertainment on the touchline at matches, wandering onto the pitch several times to share a joke with match officials.

Pictures: Mike Capps/ www.kappasport.co.uk

Right: Gascoigne was at his best when he was mixing with the community. With Paul Davis (right) he took the FA Cup to schools in Kettering, where the children adored him and his eyes moistened as he spoke of his own Cup Final misery.

Picture: Pete Norton

Gascoigne had little opportunity to kick a ball during his time at Kettering because of the latest of his 29 operations. He revealed that the simple act of heading a ball could have left him paralysed.

Pictures: Mike Capps/ www.kappasport.co.uk

Above: The relationship between chairman Imraan Ladak and manager Gascoigne rapidly disintegrated amidst a welter of allegations concerning alcohol, new signings and team selections.

Pictures: Mike Capps/www.kappasport.co.uk

Below: Kettering's fans were thrilled when Gascoigne arrived as manager, and many turned out to watch the takeover press conference through the social club windows.

Pictures: Mike Capps/www.kappasport.co.uk

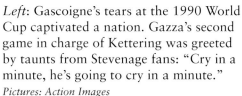

Left: Gascoigne's tears at the 1990 World Cup captivated a nation. Gazza's second game in charge of Kettering was greeted by taunts from Stevenage fans: "Cry in a minute, he's going to cry in a minute."

Pictures: Action Images

Right: His flute-playing goal celebration while a player with Glasgow Rangers caused a storm of protest among Catholics in Scotland. He was forced to apologise.

Pictures: Action Images

Below left: The Kettering players re-enacted Gascoigne's infamous dentist's chair celebration at Euro '96 (*right*), when Neil Midgley scored for Kettering in the FA Cup against Stevenage.

Pictures: Mike Capps/www.kappasport.co.uk and PA Photos

The strain of football management quickly told on Gascoigne (*above*), who crumbled under the pressure. The day after George Best's death he wore an armband in memory of his good friend, but all that could be found was a captain's band with the letter 'C' heavily prominent. Gascoigne's reign ended with all sorts of allegations about his drinking, including falling off the team bus drunk. Some fans stood up for him with a show of support at Alfreton the day after his sacking (*below*) – this was only a few hours after he had been released from a police cell, having been arrested for striking a photographer.

Pictures: Mike Capps/www.kappasport.co.uk

luck stories. Most of the time, all they wanted was money. When Gascoigne was due at the club to sign memorabilia, Mallinger claims that more often than not he failed to turn up. 'Had Paul stayed sober, he would have been such an asset, but as an alcoholic he was a nightmare.'

It was a similar story after matches at Rockingham Road, when Mallinger would go to the manager's office to ask Gascoigne to make the presentations to the sponsors. "Sometimes it would be, "Yeah, let's do it," and he'd be straight out. Other times it would just be, "Piss off."

'Had Imraan brought Paul to the club in a promotional role, and maybe as director of football rather than manager, I think Paul would still have been there now. There is no doubt he was a terrific attraction and everyone wanted a piece of him. The pressure of a manager's job was just too much for him. Imraan was so close to getting it right but he could do nothing about Paul's drink problem. And, whatever Paul says, you can't drink a double brandy if you're an alcoholic.'

With an FA Trophy third qualifying round tie against Gainsborough Trinity to play at Rockingham Road on Saturday, 26 November, the one ray of hope was that a return to home soil after three desperate games on the road might encourage a performance to settle the players and help refocus minds.

But little went to plan, and the days leading up to that match were to be dominated by blanket TV coverage of the imminent death of George Best. The past few weeks had taken a savage toll on Gascoigne, but the demise of Best, who Gascoigne claimed as a very close personal friend, was to tip him over the edge as far as his managerial career was concerned.

10

THE DEATH OF GEORGE BEST

THE POINT of no return for Gascoigne, the moment when it became obvious his days with Kettering Town were strictly numbered, was the death of George Best.

It was little surprise that Gascoigne felt a strong affinity with the Irishman, who died on Friday, 25 November at the age of 59 as a result of his alcoholism, and they had more than a drink problem in common. Best had been a Manchester United legend, and he was just 22 when he scored in the European Cup final of 1966 against Benfica to help United become the first English team to lift the trophy.

His rise to stardom came in the Swinging Sixties, when there were plenty of distractions for the superstar footballer with the film-star looks dubbed 'the fifth Beatle'. He quit Manchester United at the age of 27 and, as alcohol took a grip, over the years he became as famous for his exploits off the pitch as he had been for his footballing prowess. He received a three-month jail sentence in 1984 for drink-driving, assaulting a police officer and failing to answer bail, and spent that Christmas in Ford Open Prison.

Increasingly unable to curb his drinking, he made a now infamous appearance on BBC chat show *Wogan* in 1990, when he was clearly drunk, telling the host, 'Terry, I like screwing.' A controversial liver transplant in 2002 was followed by his being pictured in the national press drinking white wine spritzers, and, in 2004, he was again convicted of a drink-driving offence and banned for 20 months.

It was in that year that his second wife, Alex Best, went on the ITV reality show *I'm A Celebrity... Get Me Out Of Here* to tell a television audience of millions that Best had been violent towards her during their marriage. It was easy to see why Gascoigne could relate to the man many acclaim as the best British footballer of all time.

Best's death was a lingering one. On 5 October, he had been admitted to a London hospital and rushed to intensive care with a kidney infection, caused by the side-effects of immuno-suppressive drugs to prevent his body rejecting his transplanted liver. On 27 October, two days before Gascoigne became Kettering manager, it was revealed that Best was close to death and he sent a farewell message to his loved ones. Despite a small improvement in his condition, the *News of the World* carried a picture of Best in his hospital bed on 20 November, at the footballing legend's own request. His final message was: 'Don't die like me.'

Best was to hang on for a few more days, but, by the following Thursday, TV reporters camped outside the Cromwell Hospital suggested his death was imminent. The reports were relentless and gloomy, and Gascoigne's eyes welled up as he frequently glanced at the television set in the sponsors' lounge.

Some people around the club questioned how Gascoigne could have been so badly affected by the death of Best and quite how close they were, given the 20-year age gap and

Best having spent his final years in London. However, I spent time with Gascoigne on the eve of Best's death, when we watched updates which added little to the previous ones, and I can only say that Gascoigne was genuinely distressed and very emotional. Although he didn't smoke that afternoon, he was shaking. He toyed with a packet of cigarettes, shredding two into an ashtray.

Jon Dunham was with me as we spoke, with Billingham there to keep a close eye on Gascoigne. Initially, we skirted around the issue of Best, but there was no getting away from the man whose face dominated the television set on the wall. With tears in his eyes, Gascoigne struggled to put into words his emotions. As a football fan who had followed England home and away in my younger days, and who had held Gascoigne up as the most exciting talent in the English game after seeing him tear Czechoslovakia apart in a 1990 World Cup warm-up, it was unnerving.

He was so vulnerable that a big part of me wanted to wrap my arms around him and give him a cuddle. A smaller part felt embarrassed to be sitting before a man who had been my favourite English footballer of all time, watching him break up. Dunham, too, felt uncomfortable and I was glad he was able to lead the conversation as we spoke about Best.

'It is very sad, but what a bloke – all that he had to put up with, a life of being tortured by the press, the national ones who followed him round,' Gascoigne mused, before briefly brightening up as he described Best the footballer. 'He was one of the best players in the world, if not *the* best player when he was in his prime. He set football alight in this country. He was the ultimate player. You ask any of the players who played with him, ask Bobby Charlton or Denis Law. He was world class. He had a great career and lived life to the full. I don't think he'd change his life for anything.'

Then, tellingly, and perhaps indicative of why Gascoigne felt such affinity with Best, he added, 'As a man, what he had to put up with the last 40 years, it's been horrendous. It took its toll, and what a shame. But I love him. He'll be remembered by many, many people who understand football.'

Trying to talk to Gascoigne about anything else was tough. The forthcoming Saturday fixture against Gainsborough seemed hopelessly irrelevant. But Gascoigne gathered himself sufficiently to reveal how he wanted to make more signings.

This was the day it became obvious his relationship with Ladak was at breaking point. The chairman questioned much of what his manager was doing, while Gascoigne was complaining about Ladak coming into his office to challenge him over playing matters. He felt Ladak had no right to ask him to justify himself, even if the chairman was not the only one bemused by all that was happening. For the first time, Gascoigne spoke openly about Ladak, and there were clearly some tensions between the pair.

Gascoigne said, 'He fancied a player [Ryan-Zico Black] and wanted to bring him in and I said, "Yeah, OK." He'd been watching him for about three or four months.

'But I'm the manager. That's my position. I'm the one who brings in players. That's my job. I'm the one who organises things around the club. The chairman has got a good knowledge of football. I call him the young Ken Bates. But it will be me who brings in the players.'

The reference to the former Chelsea chairman, a strong-willed and forceful leader who had a reputation for being a bruiser, clearly wasn't meant as a compliment.

Ladak had concerns of his own, as it became increasingly difficult to cover up Gascoigne's drinking, which had become an open secret within the club and the subject of relentless gossip outside it. Many of the allegations were, no doubt, exaggerated as they were passed on, but Ladak had seen enough with his own eyes. Even Gascoigne, despite strenuous denials after his dismissal, was later to admit he had indeed been drinking, even if he seemed to want credit for having replaced 'four bottles of whisky' with 'the odd glass of wine'.

Although Gascoigne and Ladak had got on fine in the weeks leading up to the takeover, they had not spent enough time in each other's company to really get to know what made the other tick. They had only met for the first time three months earlier and, although they had common goals for the football club, they could not have been any more different as people.

Gascoigne liked to think of himself as a dapper dresser and took as much care over his appearance as possible. He was always clean-shaven, with his thinning hair well groomed. Ladak, while he could dress with the best when the occasion called for it, was just as happy in jeans or casual wear and could happily go a day or two without a shave. Peter Mallinger had implemented a strict jacket-and-tie dress code for the boardroom, but Ladak quickly ditched that, which irritated Gascoigne, who even suggested getting sponsored suits for everyone at the club, although nothing came of that.

To some at the club, it seemed incongruous that Gascoigne – who was seemingly oblivious to offence caused by his own behaviour, such as his occasional spitting on the floor in the boardroom and the sponsors' lounge, and his bad language – could be so troubled over someone else's choice of clothing. But he clearly fretted over Ladak not wearing what he called 'appropriate gear', just as many in the boardroom were perturbed by Gascoigne's behaviour in front of their wives.

'At a football club you get used to a fair amount of bad language but Paul was something else,' says Mallinger. 'His language was peppered with the F-word, it was always "F" this and "F" that, and even when he spoke normally about a subject there were dozens of F-words embroidering the conversation. It mattered little what company he was in. Some people got really upset with him but in many cases, rightly or wrongly, people accepted it because of who he was.'

But Ladak's dress sense wasn't the only issue on Gascoigne's mind. Ladak, a young man himself, enjoyed being among the players and went on the coaches to away games. He was a keen card player who liked playing for money, and, according to the team, he would keep going for as long as they kept their interest. While Gascoigne was happy for his players to pass time playing cards, he did not like them playing for money even if the stakes were small, knowing from experience that a player who had lost might not be in the best frame of mind for the match.

Some of the more experienced players agreed. One told me how he lost £200 on the way to an away game. When the coach arrived at its destination, he was marched off to a cashpoint by the winning player to withdraw the money. 'My head was all over the place,' he said. 'I couldn't concentrate on the game. If I was a manager, the first rule I'd bring in is no playing cards for money on the way to a game. It does your head in.'

Gascoigne claimed that Ladak had asked Paul Davis if he would help him get his FA coaching badges. There is also the disputed issue of Ladak's alleged involvement in squad matters, with Ladak denying that he said who to sign, pick or leave out, and Gascoigne insisting that he did.

Gascoigne alleges that Ladak told him which players to include for reserve-team matches. 'On the way to watch the reserves, Imraan rang up the reserve-team manager and said drop the two forwards that the manager had included and told him to play his own choice of forwards. The reserves were set up for us to take a look at new players and he totally undermined the football-management decisions. Myself and Paul Davis could not organise training sessions because we didn't know which players he wanted to add.'

The players say that, although Ladak did pop his head around the dressing-room door, it was normally only to wish them good luck. 'Imraan came in the changing room a few times but didn't say anything important,' says Diuk.

'Imraan was just one of the lads,' recalls Hall. 'He came on the coach and played cards. We talked, but only about things in general.'

Ladak had spent more than he had anticipated propping up the club in those first few weeks, but he was prepared to back moves to bring in new players. However, he had given up on getting the £50,000 from Gascoigne and, as a successful businessman, was much more aware than his manager of the need to keep outgoings within touching distance of income. He had quickly accepted that bankrolling the club was going to be his responsibility. While Mitre had handed over two pairs of boots and shinpads to the players, and the club had secured new footballs, most of the sponsorship deals they were hoping for had yet to come to fruition.

The build-up to the FA Trophy clash with Gainsborough Trinity was dominated by dissent between chairman and manager, discord in the dressing room and the effect on Gascoigne of George Best's death. And matters took a turn for the worse on the day of the game. The attendance was a disappointing 1,132, although Gascoigne's longstanding Geordie mate Chris Waddle and the former boxer Dave 'Boy' Green were in the crowd to offer support. Gascoigne's nerves had been further affected by a bust-up with Christian

Moore, who was dropped from the 16-man squad after speaking out.

Immediately before kick-off, Gascoigne, Davis and the rest of the staff had joined the players on the pitch for a minute's silence to remember Best. Gascoigne had placed an armband on the left sleeve of his jacket. The tribute had been hastily arranged and he wore a black captain's armband featuring a prominent letter 'C'.

Poppies won 1–0, thanks to a Neil Midgley goal after just five minutes, but the performance was a disappointment against a physical Gainsborough side who made life as difficult as possible. 'It was the same against most of the teams we played,' recalls Andy Hall. 'They knew we had Gazza and managers were saying things to their players like, "These are big-time Charlies and we need to get into their faces." They were going out thinking this was their cup final and they didn't need much of a team-talk. They were up for it.'

Gascoigne again strayed on to the pitch during the game. One moment he was lively and animated, the next distracted. Even the referee pointed out that Gascoigne did not seem 'in quite the right state to be on the line'. Gascoigne attributed his erratic behaviour to medication, not alcohol, citing the effects of the detox medication Librium.

Those who had been in the boardroom with Gascoigne before kick-off say he had again been drinking brandy, and it seems nobody saw him eat anything. He had a cup of coffee with him at the side of the pitch, but this had been topped up with brandy, and even before half-time it was obvious there was a problem.

'How in control of it was he?' Hall rhetorically asks. 'Did he know how much he was drinking? I was 19, I wasn't the one to go up to him and say, "Look you've drunk too much." He was the manager. You'd like to think he knew what he was doing but only he really knows whether he was in control or not.'

Clearly, the half-time team talk was little better. 'When he hadn't had a drink he was the nicest man you'd ever meet,' adds Hall. 'Even when he'd had a bit he was nice, but then he could talk a lot of rubbish. It's difficult. He's slurring his words but I suppose it could be for any reason.'

Gascoigne left it to Paul Davis to face the press after the game. Billingham, whose two young sons had been mascots, had his family with him, so Gascoigne was driven straight off by the local commercial radio station to Kettering town centre to switch on the town's Christmas lights. While Davis tried to put a brave face on a disappointing display, admitting, 'It is still not quite where we want it to be,' a flushed-looking Gascoigne took to the stage in the Market Place.

He stood alongside the likes of Scooby Doo and Wicky Bear, the mascot of the local Wicksteed Park, and beamed when he was cheered by a crowd in its hundreds, although it was later alleged he was drunk and had sworn at a child asking for an autograph.

Afterwards, he returned to the social club at Rockingham Road, where he continued to drink while playing pool.

By now, Gascoigne was close to breaking point. The next day, after drinking white wine while signing photographs, he'd had enough. Leaving his dad and Jimmy Five Bellies in the hotel bar, he walked out of the front door and ordered a minicab. He paid the driver £300 to take him to Leeds, and later said he checked into a bed-and-breakfast, spending the night alone. He caught a train back to Kettering the following day.

'Paul was continuing to drink and the worse the results the more he drank,' Mallinger says. 'Catch him early on and he would be pleasant enough. Right from the start he made a point of kissing everyone the moment he arrived and again before kick-off. On a match day at Rockingham Road, we seldom saw him after the game. He just disappeared into his office with the brandy. Paul Davis drove him back to his hotel or the health farm. I can't think what they made of that.'

Although Ladak would later reflect that perhaps more should have been done to support Gascoigne, he was concerned at the time that Kettering's season was plunging irretrievably towards the bottom half of the table. As chairman, he had obligations to the supporters whose expectations he had helped raise and who were beginning to complain about performances. There had also been dismay at the sudden departure of the popular Paterson.

Despite the win over Gainsborough, many were not convinced about the direction their team was heading in. Some were dismissive of the way in which the players laboured to implement the Gascoigne/Davis masterplan, which had not been helped by a muddy, bobbly pitch and tough physical opponents who had got stuck in from the first whistle. Jon Dunham noted in his match report that at times the match was 'downright awful', the only highlight of which was scraping into the next round.

'They changed the whole structure of the side. What we had thought we were doing well, we obviously weren't, and that was all about shape,' says Diuk. 'Things just got worse and worse. It got to a point where Paul Davis ended up telling us to stop playing and start knocking the ball into the corners. That was against all his beliefs.'

Davis, always the diplomat, said in his post-match interview that he had felt the pressure of recent weeks, but went out of his way to praise the townsfolk, the great people around the club who give their time voluntarily and 'some very passionate fans'. But, even though the victory eased the pressure a little, there were plenty asking whether the game was up.

Dave Dunham says he took no pleasure in seeing his doubts realised. It had been obvious to him from the outset that Gascoigne was not the right man. 'It was a sham. If everything about Gascoigne had been absolutely right, then he would not have been looking to manage Kettering Town. In today's world, if you're a top-flight footballer at the highest level and you're sound in most other departments, then you go straight in and manage a Premier League club. Gareth Southgate or Alan Shearer or Gianfranco Zola don't manage the likes of Kettering. Which footballer who played at the highest level has moved through the ranks of non-League football? The only one who springs to mind is Martin O'Neill, perhaps Nigel Clough. But they didn't play at the level of Gascoigne and they are very, very rare.

'Gascoigne was flawed. Perhaps he felt that coming to Kettering as manager would draw him back into the football spotlight, which I'm sure he courted and which I'm sure he missed. Gascoigne needed people to be interested in him. I just wonder why we as a nation have this celebrity cult thing. He's just a flawed man who could play football.'

Gascoigne's flaws may have been obvious, but few took pleasure in his downfall. Diuk points the finger of blame at the new management's insistence on changing everything that had previously stood them in good stead, but says of Gascoigne, 'I was never angry with him. How could I be? He had too many problems. I remember going to work on a Monday morning and looking at a paper. He was on the front page being drunk. All my workmates were laughing.'

Gascoigne met Jon Dunham on the Thursday ahead of the league clash at home to Barrow on Saturday, 3 December. He was aware that matters needed to improve on the pitch if the slide in attendances was to be halted. 'It's important we get the fans coming through the turnstiles, but you can only get that with results. It doesn't matter how cheap the hot dogs are.' He again insisted, 'We are going in the right direction without a shadow of a doubt.'

People who saw Gascoigne around the club during those 39 days remarked how his appearance and demeanour could change so much from one day to the next. One day he might be distracted, nervous, stumbling over his words and difficult to understand, and the next he would have a healthy glow and be clearer and more incisive in all he said. The Gascoigne who sat with Dunham that afternoon was very much the latter and he said he wanted to put the club's recent poor performances behind them. 'It's a big month. The leagues start to sort themselves out in January no matter what division it is. We can't be slipping up at home against teams in the lower half.'

With Davis and a fitness expert brought in from Northampton University, he had put the players through a series of physical tests that he said had produced impressive results. 'But the key is the warm-up,' he told Dunham. 'We don't want to deal with any pulls or little strains.' He seemed to want to demonstrate that he was in control of all the small details that go together to build a progressive club.

On 1 December, the *Evening Telegraph* carried a four-page Kettering Town pull-out entitled 'Here's To The Future'. There was no sense of irony to the title, and the pages produced by the newspaper's advertising department told readers how rosy everything was at Rockingham Road.

Billingham had penned the introduction, and it had the usual waffle about full-time players, new ground and getting into the Football League. It also revealed plans to introduce Xbox games to complement skittles and pool in the social club.

He went on to explain how the club was 'attracting interest from Italy to Russia, from Hong Kong to America', and he knew why: 'The whole of the UK is looking for Kettering's results at 4.50pm on a Saturday afternoon to see how Gazza's team are getting on. He is a national treasure who is loved by millions.'

Unfortunately, there was little time left for this national treasure to keep the world entertained with his antics at Kettering Town. By 1 December, his future at the club was numbered in days.

11

GASCOIGNE
SACKED

ALTHOUGH Gascoigne's sacking as manager was announced on the afternoon of Monday 5 December, there were whispers on the day before that he'd gone. Some of the players received phone calls over the weekend from a tearful Gascoigne telling them that Ladak was trying to sack him and asking them to stand by him. 'Are you with me?' he would repeatedly demand.

Matters had come to a head as the chairman and manager clashed following the 3–1 home defeat by Barrow on the Saturday afternoon, and the argument continued by text message into the evening.

Gascoigne, who admits to drinking white wine after the game and was also seen drinking brandy before it, sent Ladak an insulting text, telling the chairman to sack him if he didn't like the way he was running the team. Towards the end of a clearly fraught day for both parties, this was the final straw for Ladak, who was clearly angry and frustrated by Gascoigne's attitude over the previous few hours.

Although some of the players were aware of the dismissal following Gascoigne's emotional phone calls, the news was not officially released by the club until lunchtime on the Monday. But, by the time the announcement was placed on the club's website, the circle of people to whom Gascoigne was ranting about Ladak had widened considerably.

That brief statement sparked what was possibly the most incredible 48 hours in the history of Kettering Town Football Club. Few, if any, non-League clubs would have experienced anything like it, as an increasingly vitriolic public war of words raged between two stubborn men, with Sky Sports and the national and local press reporting every stage of the drama. It made compulsive viewing and reading, and many journalists were able to dust down their 'Gascoigne mucks up again' headlines.

The game which proved the breaking point took place on a bog of a pitch against Barrow, watched by a paltry 1,272, the lowest home league crowd of Gascoigne's time, with just 30 visiting supporters bothering to make the trip. But the Kettering performance wasn't the worst under Gascoigne, and his team had looked set for a point at 1–1 going into injury time at the end of 90 minutes. However, some awful Kettering defending in those final few minutes handed Barrow two shocking goals and their first league victory in almost three months.

Like many of the teams Kettering faced that autumn, Barrow weren't much more than a bunch of honest workmen. They were happy to let the home players have the ball in areas that posed no threat, but scrapped like tigers when it came anywhere near their goal. Even they couldn't claim their win was deserved, but they achieved what they set out to do. They had frustrated Kettering's attempts to play the passing game and cashed in on the silly mistakes that had become the signature mark of a team low on confidence and high on self-doubt.

Although Gascoigne had recalled fit-again centre-half

Derek Brown, he had persisted with a central midfield of defender David Theobald and winger Andy Hall. On a day when things seemed destined to go wrong on and off the pitch, he also lost striker Neil Midgley to injury after 15 minutes, forcing him to send on the transfer-listed Christian Moore as his replacement. Three of the players who had been signed on full-time deals, Dixon, McKenzie and Fowler, started on the bench while Ryan-Zico Black missed out completely because of injury. The exclusion of the new signings proved a particular frustration for Ladak.

For Gascoigne, another performance in which his players had failed to implement his expansive game plan and then conceded two late goals could not have come on a worse day. George Best's funeral service had finished only a short time before kick-off and had clearly affected Gascoigne, who had watched the emotionally charged events in Belfast live on television. He then asked his team to go out and win the game for his good friend being buried in Northern Ireland.

'Before the game it was easy to see that there was a strain on his face and it was the one and only time that I saw him have a drink,' says Black, who watched events unfold from the stand.

Diuk passed the manager's office before the game, and through the open door saw Gascoigne drinking what he was sure was a glass of brandy. Other players agree it was obvious that Gascoigne had been drinking when he came into the dressing room to announce the team. 'He was drunk before that game,' claims Brett Solkhon. 'He just wasn't coping. He needed a break from it all; he needed somebody to put their arm around him.'

Davis quickly ran through what was expected of them, which was pretty much the same as for previous games, although many of the players were barely listening. 'He was a nice bloke but for me he had nothing about him,' recalls

Diuk. 'I didn't think he had much of a personality, he was like a robot.'

'I had stopped listening by then, I had switched off,' Moore admits. 'Anything could have been happening. It could have been a juggler coming in to play centre-half for all I knew. The lads had got to the point where it was, God knows what's going to happen next. All I knew was that if I got man of the match I was going to get to drive a Lamborghini for a week!'

After the sorry match, the Kettering players returned to their dressing room to lick their wounds, while Gascoigne and Davis headed back to their office and a bitterly frustrated Ladak went to find Gascoigne. As chairman, he wanted answers to questions that he felt could no longer be avoided: why was the manager persisting in playing players out of position? Why was he picking ones whose confidence was so damaged they were a liability to the team? What were his plans for the new signings? And, on a personal level, what was he going to do about his drinking?

He was also concerned how the poor performances and results were impacting on attendances. His own expectations, already high, had been further raised by the surge of enthusiasm surrounding the Stevenage game, and he didn't like the way crowds were falling away.

'Imraan had gone to the manager's office only to find Paul heavily under the influence,' recalls Peter Mallinger. 'Paul Davis was just sitting there. Imraan was upset with them both as he had previously asked Paul Davis to try to ensure that Paul kept off the drink, but he was nothing like strong enough to have any effect on Paul. He had an impossible task, and I do not think there was anything anyone could do.'

Ladak continued to pose questions that Gascoigne wouldn't answer, except to snap back that it was up to him as manager who did and didn't play. Gascoigne told Ladak that Kettering were sixth in the table and still in a good position to go up, but Ladak was having none of it. He had seen every minute of the matches under their stewardship and knew for himself how fragile matters were in the dressing room.

Mallinger believed Gascoigne seemed intent on destroying himself in the same way as George Best had done, claiming it was obvious to everybody at the club that Gascoigne was fighting a losing battle against the bottle and that his position as manager had become untenable. 'Once you have lost that respect in the dressing room it becomes an impossible situation,' states Mallinger. 'Several players had told me they wanted to get away as quickly as possible because they could see what was happening and wanted no part of it.'

Supporters who had been so dazzled by the bright star that had lit up Kettering were now grumbling about a slide down the table. Although few really turned on Gascoigne, many were disturbed by the rumours rife in the town, which sadly were only confirmed by what they were seeing at matches.

With all this weighing on his shoulders, Ladak felt he had to take decisive action to prevent a sorry situation becoming even worse. 'Paul couldn't stop at one and his heavy drinking before and after a game made any type of logical discussion impossible,' testifies Mallinger.

After walking out of Gascoigne's office, Ladak found Mallinger and asked him if he knew whether Kevin Wilson had found another club. Mallinger said he was pretty sure he hadn't, although, shortly after his departure a month earlier, Wilson had been offered a coaching position in Holland, but he had decided against it to save uprooting his young family from their Northampton home. He was doing a bit of Saturday-afternoon commentary for BBC Radio Northampton but, other than that, was not involved in football.

Gascoigne left the ground and returned to the Kettering Park Hotel, where he continued to drink and fret over what had passed between himself and Ladak. Unaware that Ladak was already trying to track Wilson down to offer him the chance to return, Gascoigne sent a text to the chairman accusing him of being a 'control freak'. He also told Ladak that, if he didn't like what he was doing, he should sack him. Ladak telephoned Billingham to tell him he'd lost faith in Gascoigne's ability to manage with a clear head and he was dismissed. He called Wilson and they agreed to meet the next day.

*   *   *

Gascoigne had been in no mood, or state, to speak to the press after the match, and Davis was sent out to field questions about their team's woeful collapse. He gave as honest an assessment as he had delivered during his time as Gascoigne's second in command, blaming poor defending and silly mistakes, although he also accused Barrow of 'killing the game from start to finish'.

Jon Dunham, who posed the questions, recalls, 'He didn't look me in the eye once. I was trying to make eye contact and you could see that he'd had enough. He was a decent man.'

Ollie Burgess, one of the casualties of Gascoigne's mix 'n' match policy but the Poppies' man of the match in this game, said the day had been 'frustrating for the lads'. It was one in a growing list.

The players set off for home seemingly unaware of the spat between chairman and manager, but it wasn't long before they began to hear whispers that everything was about to change. 'I went home very disappointed,' says Diuk. 'Then Mooro rang up and said he'd heard Gascoigne had been sacked. I put Sky Sports News on but it said nothing about it.'

Andy Hall also set off for home and when his mobile rang he was surprised to find a clearly distressed Gascoigne on the line. 'He was in tears, saying, "I'm going to be sacked." I'm sure he was drunk and he was very upset. He was throwing out comments like, "Don't sign for them," and "Get out while you can," and telling me he'd take me to this and that club. I didn't really know what to say. What can you say? For me, it wasn't that unexpected. Things were being said and with all the drinking and everything else it hardly came out of the blue.'

Hall's burning ambition at the time was to play in the Football League, having had a taste of the good life with Coventry. He had tried to put all the distractions behind him to concentrate on his own job but it was difficult. 'A lot of the time he was out of it when he was talking, and that's a shame for me to say because he was one of my heroes when I was growing up,' he recalls. 'Sometimes I wanted to say something but I was more shy than anything. I didn't know how he'd react.'

It was a confusing couple of days for the players. Brett Solkhon says that among the rumours flying around that weekend was the story that Gascoigne had bought the club and Ladak had left. 'We were hearing all sorts of things. Then he rang me at about five o'clock on the Sunday afternoon absolutely paralytic. I've been drunk before but I don't think I've ever been *that* drunk.

'He was slurring his words so badly that I could barely understand what he was saying. He told me that Imraan wanted to sack him but that Kettering Town was his club and that he was going to get him out. He kept asking me, "Are you with me, Brett?" over and over again. He was telling me how he was getting the players together to take over the club.

'I agreed with him at the time because he wasn't in a good state. He needed help.'

Another player to speak to Gascoigne on the telephone after his dismissal was Diuk. Although he had been tipped off about the sacking, by Monday morning he had heard nothing. 'I thought, "Sod it, I'll ring him." First of all I spoke to Andy Billingham because you could never get straight through to Gazza, it always had to be through someone else. I asked him what was going on, and Andy said, as far as Paul was concerned, he would be at the game the next day as normal. The next thing is Gazza's ripped the phone out of Andy's hand and he's just ranting down the phone at me, ranting and ranting about Imraan and how he's been shit on. He said to me, "My other phone is ringing and it's some model bird who wants to take me out on a date but I'd rather speak to you." I'm just sat there with my missus on the bed, and I put the phone on loud speaker. He went on and on. He said, "I'll be there Tuesday."'

Gascoigne was well clear of Kettering when he spoke to Diuk, having travelled to Birmingham on the Sunday to stay with Billingham ahead of a charity event in Liverpool the following day. He couldn't accept he was being sacked.

After the conversation with Diuk, Billingham telephoned me. I was at home on a day off when I took the call shortly before Ladak posted his statement on the Poppies website. Billingham was telling me the events of the previous 36 hours, when Gascoigne snatched the phone from him and started ranting at me: 'The chairman wants to sack me ... I said I'd never walk away ... I'll fight all the way ... I'm now looking to buy the football club ... I'll never walk away ... I said I'd achieve League status in three to five years.'

Gascoigne accused Ladak of many things, including not talking to visiting directors and sponsors, and alleged he had 'never been left alone to do my job as manager ... I have spoken to top professionals in the game and they said I should've walked away. I didn't and got my head down and

I will stick in there. If the fans want to get rid of me I'll take that on board. I haven't been paid. Imraan questioned Paul Davis's decision on Arsenal reserve-team players, saying, "Are they good enough to play for Kettering Town?" He sacked a longstanding fan and supporter of the club and I reinstated him. I paid all the voluntary staff out of my own pocket. Imraan's view was: don't pay them because they're not used to it.'

There was plenty more where that came from.

Billingham eventually managed to retrieve the phone from Gascoigne and told me, 'That's all off the record!'

I laughed. A few hours later, Gascoigne went live on Sky Sports News to not only repeat those claims, but also throw in a whole lot more.

If Ladak had been caught out by the media frenzy that had accompanied Gascoigne's appointment as manager, he must have been overwhelmed by the explosive reaction to his latest decision.

The official statement was kept deliberately brief. Ladak told Billingham and Gascoigne that he would not make public the reasons behind his decision if the personal attacks on him that Monday stopped. However, Ladak felt the need to respond to what he saw as the string of libellous accusations that Gascoigne had made against him on Sky Sports News that evening. It was an interview that revealed to football fans everywhere what many in Kettering had seen for themselves. He was rambling, repetitive and his speech was slurred. He struggled to find words to express his pain and outrage. It was very, very sad.

In contrast, Ladak won a lot of respect for his measured response. Although Gascoigne later insisted he was not drunk during the interview, he did admit to drinking 'two or three' glasses of wine at the fundraising event for a drug and alcohol treatment centre in Liverpool. He claimed that he only *appeared* drunk and that he was in an 'emotional state and shaking' because he was taking medication that reacted with even one glass of wine. He was also deeply distressed at his unfair sacking.

Whether he was drunk or not, he was unable to stop himself launching another verbal assault on Ladak, claiming he had interfered with team affairs, signed his own players and said who should be playing in the reserves – much of which he had alleged in earlier phone conversations with me. He also declared the players were behind him, the staff were behind him, the town of Kettering was behind him. 'The unfortunate thing is the chairman isn't.'

The dam had been breached, and there was no stopping him. 'As far as I'm concerned I'm not sacked because I've never signed a contract. I am going to continue with my director of football Andy Billingham and my financial adviser to buy Kettering Town Football Club. I am not walking away. I stuck by my own guns. I stuck with how football should be played, I stuck by the players. He told the players he'd be giving them professional contracts and 10 days later he's wanting me to get rid of them.'

Gascoigne decided to disregard Ladak's position and appealed to the club's supporters. 'The fans can make their own decision. They either want me and Paul Davis to take this club forward or they want a doctor in charge. He has my whole staff a nervous wreck and I can't continue in this way. If I do leave, then God bless Kettering Town Football Club and the next manager.'

While Gascoigne ranted and raved, Ladak calmly rebutted the charges and started to explain why he had made his decision.

'Unfortunately, Paul Gascoigne has been under the influence of alcohol before, during and after several first-team games and training sessions,' he said. 'I have tried to help Paul through this difficult period but I gave an undertaking to the board prior to my takeover that if Paul hit the bottle I would remove him as manager. Paul has not reacted well to the news and has made numerous threats that if I do not sell him the club he will use his name and the media to turn supporters against me. This has already begun with Paul calling a number of first-team players under the influence of alcohol.

'I have not interfered with team selection or player purchases and departures. But I have been disappointed with the way two players in particular have been treated by Paul. I also made clear that I felt Paul had turned a winning team into a confused and unsettled one by playing players out of position and being drunk on the team bus and in the dressing room.'

Ladak had told Gascoigne not to go public with his allegations, and felt they required a rebuttal. 'All I want is for Paul to seek professional medical assistance for his addictions and to stop taking his frustration out by trying to unsettle this club further. I would also like to make clear that I told Paul I would not bring any of this into the public domain unless I was forced to do so. Paul is not a shareholder or director of Kettering Town Football Club.'

The charge that really stung Ladak was that he had interfered in team affairs. Having spent the autumn close to him, he felt he understood why so much had gone wrong in Gascoigne's life. 'I lost confidence that Paul was making decisions with a clear mind. Unfortunately, it did not work out for him at Boston, and I believed Paul's version of events. It didn't work out in Portugal, and I believed Paul's version of events. It did not work out in China and I believed Paul's version of events. And it didn't work out for Paul here and I don't believe his version of events.

'It sounds like the same old stories, like him saying he

hasn't been paid, he has been interfered with and promises were broken. But I kept my side. I told the fans I would run this club in the best interests of Kettering Town. I could have stuck with it and gambled with the football club. I could have stuck by my decision to bring him in as manager out of pride. I am disappointed with the way things have gone. I didn't want to be in a public slanging match but I have had to come out and defend myself and the club. It's been horrible. Really, really horrible.'

As for the allegation that he had tried to pick the team, Ladak said, 'Paul joked around and asked me to guess the team the night before a game. Sometimes I would get it right, sometimes I would get it wrong. I just gave Paul my opinion as chairman and said he could either take it on board or leave it. But playing players out of position has unsettled the squad.'

Ladak hoped the Sky Sports News interview would be an end of the matter, saying, 'I hope we can draw a line under all this because it is certainly not good for the football club and it is not good for Paul.'

However, Gascoigne was insistent he was going to turn up at the next day's game, away to Alfreton, despite Wilson accepting Ladak's invitation to return as manager. Gascoigne said he would shout instructions to 'my players' over the head of Wilson in the dug-out if necessary. Again, he appealed to the fans to help him overthrow Ladak. 'I love Kettering. I love the fans, I love everybody involved in Kettering. There will either be me in the club or him. If I leave, that depends on the fans. If the fans want me to leave, then I will hold my hands up like a man, like a proper man, not make excuses.'

But Gascoigne was out of touch with the mood of the majority of supporters, who were fed up at their team's performances. Many were also concerned that their club was becoming a bit of a joke. Although a handful tried to show their support for the sacked manager at Alfreton, they were drowned out by the majority, who gave their backing to Ladak. They had a growing list of complaints and many had been upset to see the popular Jamie Paterson sent packing.

One fan said, 'It is a soap opera. We have gone from "We are going to rise" to being a laughing stock. He [Gascoigne] did not really endear himself to most people. A lot of people thought he was worse for wear a lot of the time.'

Another supporter admitted that releasing Paterson had upset a lot of the longstanding fans. 'I thought it would only be a matter of time,' he revealed. 'You heard different stories.'

Dave Dunham summed up local feeling. 'People had been excited by Gascoigne's appointment, the gates had gone up and they felt the club had been put on the map. But it was now in the spotlight for all the wrong reasons.'

Despite everything, there was little anger directed at Gascoigne personally. He never received any of the abuse or taunts that other football managers have endured when things have gone wrong. Perhaps supporters felt that he wasn't entirely responsible for his own actions.

Kevin Meikle said, 'Many fans of other non-League clubs were sceptical and most were discussing how long it would be before the club would part company with Paul. I didn't share their enthusiasm to see the journey end early. I, like many, wanted everything to work out not only for the club, but also for Gascoigne. It is obvious that there is a lot of feeling for him in football and in the public domain.'

Peter Mallinger was impressed with the way Ladak stood up to the attacks on him. 'Imraan knew his decision to sack Paul would kick off another media circus but he also knew that to continue would have damaged the club for years to come. He made a brave decision. Everything Imraan said was true. I can vouch for it because I was so close to it.'

Mallinger also says that some of Gascoigne's allegations

were particularly hurtful for Ladak because, with only gate receipts and a small bonus from the FA Cup, 'it became a lot more expensive than he thought it would be. It hurt him when Paul went but he stuck at it. It wasn't easy for him, and it wasn't cheap.'

That afternoon, Jon Dunham telephoned as many players as possible, all of whom had been instructed not to talk to the press. Derek Brown said, 'It's a big shock for all of us. The club contacted us to say we shouldn't make any comment.'

Others were more willing to speak but, in the confusion, had little to add. At that stage, they clearly had no idea what was coming next.

The players turned up at club that evening to find Wilson already there. 'I'm back on a three-year contract,' he told them, before quickly laying down the law. The Gascoigne era was over. 'You can forget all the big ideas and fancy plans, things are going to change.'

Although the four new signings wanted to know how they fitted in, Wilson wanted to get back to the basics he knew the bulk of the squad were familiar with. 'Yeah, you could play the ball around against the footballing sides in the Northern Conference, but there were very few of them,' he claimed. 'You've got to play two ways in the Northern Conference – you've got to be physically strong and you've got to get it up to your front men. I believe you can go and play football in their half, but you don't try to knock it around at the back. The Northern Conference is not the place for people to play fancy football. These boys are strong, they are tough, they get into your face and they make it hard for you.'

It seemed Wilson was as keen as Ladak to put events of the past six weeks behind the club.

'We had turned up not knowing who was going to be there,' recalls Diuk. 'Then I saw Kev, and I started to think everything would be all right again.'

Andy Hall agrees. 'When Kev came back, it was like nothing had happened.'

One of Wilson's priorities on his return was to call Jamie Paterson and ask him back as player-coach. Wilson was out to replicate what had worked so well before, while Paterson hoped to rebuild shattered team spirit and confidence. 'Most of the lads have been at sixes and sevens over the past month or so and didn't really know whether they were coming or going. I am disappointed with the way Paul Gascoigne conducted himself. I am like everyone else, I grew up idolising the man for his footballing ability. But not for so many other things he has done in his life.'

Wilson, Paterson, the players and most of the supporters hoped that the circus, as it was widely referred to, had moved on. They wanted to get back to playing football in their own relative peace and quiet.

The game at Alfreton was the rearranged fixture after the match a month earlier had been rained off, to Gascoigne's annoyance. But even if the hope was that the circus had packed up and hit the road, there was still Gascoigne's insistence that he was going to turn up at the Impact Arena. Gascoigne had told the players he planned to be at the game and repeated that in his rant at me. He was asked about it during his Sky Sports News interview, and replied that if he wasn't allowed in the dressing room he would stand behind the dug-out to give instructions to the players 'on how to play and how not to play'.

Gascoigne said the team would respond more to him than to Wilson, and as the team bus set off the players speculated over whether he would keep his promise. 'It was a matter of: is Gazza going to turn up?' recalls Diuk. 'He didn't. But I think Kev would have loved that. I think Kev might well have just turned round and bopped him one.'

It was just the sort of promising situation to ensure that

this small Midlands club was for a second time swamped by applications for press passes from journalists anticipating yet more Gazza-inspired histrionics. As it happened, Gascoigne never made it to Alfreton. Although he was responsible for another lot of lurid newspaper headlines long before the turnstiles were opened to those keen to see how the evening would pan out.

12

GAZZA OR THE DOCTOR?

T HE JOURNALISTS who set off for Alfreton that Tuesday afternoon had every reason to expect an even bigger story than the one they had been anticipating the night before. By the time they had taken to the M1, Gascoigne was again headline news on TV and radio. The story had taken another twist, with the sacked manager arrested and detained in a police cell in Liverpool overnight on suspicion of assault. If it was still his intention to head for the Impact Arena that evening, the number of journalists who wanted to be there to question him about the past few days was set to grow by the minute.

The irony of the alcoholic Gascoigne drinking glasses of white wine at a fundraising event for a charity dedicated to drugs and alcohol treatment wasn't lost on some. But it was no laughing matter. Gascoigne was distressed and disturbed during his interview with Sky, and never had that golden goal against Scotland in 1996 seemed further away. How could this most magical of footballers, seemingly with the world at his feet, have fallen so far that people were watching him on TV and then taking to the internet to post comments about him 'not living in the real world', being 'his own worst enemy' and claiming 'he's gone completely bananas'? One comment tried to add a bit of perspective when it urged, 'all this anger over kettering town lol, take a chill gazza.'

For Gascoigne, it wasn't just that everything at Kettering had failed, it was that things for him personally had fallen apart yet again. It hurt. He had genuinely believed this was his opportunity to make a success of the rest of his life in football, yet it had all exploded in his face after just 39 days.

Imraan Ladak had made allegations of 37 separate drink-related incidents and players had accused him of destroying the team. But when someone did stick up for him it only served to fan the flames. Gordon Taylor, chief executive of the PFA, spoke fondly of Gascoigne, and went on to complain that Ladak's revelations had been 'uncalled for given that Paul has not received a penny' as manager. Ladak retorted that Gascoigne had waived his salary for the first five months and that he had never come up with his share of the takeover cash. It seemed, at that point, that Ladak was prepared to roll up his sleeves and take on all-comers.

Despite standing his ground so well as the battle raged, Ladak could not have been looking forward to the trip to Alfreton. The potential for a confrontation with Gascoigne and another embarrassing episode in front of the media and travelling Kettering fans was not one that appealed to him. He was well aware of the affection many people had for Gascoigne despite, or perhaps even because of, all his flaws. Ladak knew there was every chance he would end up being painted as the villain of this particular chapter in Gascoigne's fall from grace. Outside Kettering few cared about the minor-league club, and the damage being done to it didn't stack up against the suffering of Paul Gascoigne.

Ladak showed his mettle that day. He could have found an excuse not to make the trip, and many in his position may have done that. But he accepted the challenge and set off for a football match that had become a sideshow. He claimed he had been threatened with physical violence, although these threats were later withdrawn, and that he was warned Gascoigne was a 'national treasure' whose name alone would turn everyone against him. He refused to say where the threats had come from, but said Gascoigne knew nothing of them.

As it turned out, the biggest danger to his physical wellbeing that evening was the media scrum that surged towards him on his arrival at Alfreton's small main stand. For the rubberneckers, it was a serious anti-climax.

Ladak was in a more conciliatory mood as he spoke ahead of the game. He had been saddened by the news of Gascoigne's arrest and night in the police cell, and had questioned himself as to whether he could have handled it all differently. It had crossed his mind to ask Gascoigne to temporarily step down to seek treatment for his alcoholism and other problems, but he believed Gascoigne was taking his advice from the wrong people.

Gascoigne had only been released from the police cell in Liverpool a few hours before Ladak arrived at Alfreton. He had been accused of assaulting a photographer as he left the charity fundraiser at around 11pm the previous evening, having spent time signing items for an auction which raised £5,000.

Chris Difford, former guitarist and songwriter with the band Squeeze, had been a guest and left at the same time, and claims he saw a posse of photographers waiting outside to ambush Gascoigne. He accused them of being more aggressive than usual as they closed in. 'It just looked like firework night. There were so many cameras going off. They were pushing and shoving and he did not want his photograph to be taken.'

Gascoigne had posed for pictures on his arrival. But, with

his emotions running high, he'd had enough. He was distressed, he had mixed alcohol with prescription drugs and the photographers who were lining the street were an obvious target. Gascoigne claimed he did no more than shove one of the photographers away, while Difford said he didn't see any contact but did see a photographer bleeding from his face. The photographer, Steve Farrell, a freelance, said he had asked Gascoigne if it was OK to take his picture and Gascoigne walked towards him. 'He made like he was going to shake my hand and said, "No, but you don't mind this, do you?" Then he whacked me with a left hand. It was a proper punch.'

Farrell, who made a complaint to police after being treated by paramedics in the street, said Gascoigne was pulled away by bystanders. 'The worst thing was Gazza just started laughing hysterically. He seemed to think it was hilarious,' he said. He later dropped the charges, although by then Gascoigne had spent the night in the cell. For somebody who lists claustrophobia among his many conditions, it must have been a difficult night.

14 hours after he was arrested and six hours before kick-off at Alfreton, Gascoigne was released to be met by Andy Billingham and John McKeown who drove him away. Later that afternoon, Billingham issued a short statement to the Press Association which said Gascoigne would not be going to Alfreton. 'I thoroughly enjoyed working with a great bunch of lads and I wish them every success under Kevin Wilson,' it quoted Gascoigne as saying.

The announcement was the main sports news headline on the radio as the team bus, supporters' coaches and media headed for the Impact Arena. While the newspaper reporters picked up their press passes and went about gathering material for their 'life after Gazza' articles, some of the TV crews were frustrated. As I arrived at the small club car park with Jon Dunham and Mike Capps, one TV crew was busy packing up to drive away. It was still over an hour before kick-off. No Gazza, no story for them, it seemed.

But there was still a story to be had for those who did stick around. Ladak and Wilson took the centre stage vacated by Gascoigne. Ladak, despite his lack of media experience, again acquitted himself well in the face of a barrage of questions. With the news that Gascoigne was no longer heading in his direction, he spoke of his concern for the man with whom he had crossed swords in the most public of spats. 'I worked very hard to make sure it didn't come out this way,' he said. 'But, unfortunately, I believe the one person who was advising Paul gave him some very bad advice.

'All I can say is that Paul was my footballing hero. I had a plan which was very much based around me and Paul working together and I would not make allegations against Paul. Everything I said, my hand was forced to come out and say. I do believe Paul needs help and, if he surrounds himself with the right people that really care about him and aren't there to make money out of him, to make cash and try to become his agent and so forth, then he will get through this and he will come back the wonderful person he is when he is completely focused.'

The person Ladak was sniping at was Billingham, who had been closest to Gascoigne during those 39 days and who left the club with him.

Paul Davis also walked away. He was as much a victim of circumstances as anybody else. He had done what he could to support Gascoigne, as well as to keep the playing side ticking over in the face of scepticism over his methods.

'They put on these very technical training sessions and it was all so different to what we were used to,' says Brett Solkhon. 'We had some good players who could definitely play a bit but you had to be realistic. You get more time in the top leagues, and they had obviously come from that.'

Wayne Diuk, one of the most experienced non-League players at the club at the time of the takeover, believes Ladak, Gascoigne and Davis were too naïve. 'I think they thought it was Championship Manager on the computer, they really did. "We'll go in there, we'll buy this player and this player and we'll be in the Premier League in a few years,"' he says. 'They couldn't grasp what it was about. The good sides at this level could play football but they could win games by being scrappy and physical and horrible. We had lads who preferred the big scraps to playing football but they tried to make us play like a Premier League club and we just weren't good enough. They squeezed the rough and tumble out of us.'

As Kettering fought out a 1–1 draw at Alfreton, few observers showed much interest in the club's prospects. Almost every question thrown at Ladak at his impromptu press conference was about his ex-manager. A handful of the club's fans had gone to the opposite end of the ground to where the majority of Kettering's support had taken up their position and had unfurled a handwritten banner on a white sheet saying, '100% GAZZA DOCTER OUT'. That was the result of Gascoigne's challenge to supporters to decide whether they wanted him, Paul Gascoigne, a professional footballer, or Imraan Ladak, a doctor, running their club. Gascoigne had continually referred to Ladak as a doctor over the previous 36 hours, and Ladak raised a laugh at the end of his chat with the press when he finished with: 'And I would just like to stress again, I am not a doctor and never have been.'

Even amid all the angst, there had been touches of humour. In his Sky interview, Gascoigne had dismissed Ladak's knowledge of football by saying, 'The guy can't trap a bag of cement as far as I'm concerned,' while another banner was placed over a pitchside advertising hoarding alongside 'DOCTER OUT' to proclaim 'FREE GAZZA OUR TOWN NEEDS YOU'. The authors of this one had obviously not been listening to the radio on their way to Alfreton.

As the Poppies players crept almost unnoticed into the dressing room to get ready for the first match of Wilson's second coming, so Gascoigne headed back to Champneys. Although he had moved out a couple of weeks previously because the health farm was gearing up for the pre-Christmas rush, the owner had called Gascoigne and offered him the chance to return. At least there he could escape all the media attention that wasn't doing him any good, even if he had been responsible for whipping up much of it himself.

Gascoigne's feelings were raw and his battle with Ladak was clouding his judgment to the extent that he refused to go into rehabilitation for his drink problem. To him, that would mean Ladak had won. As he headed off to relative obscurity for at least a short while, Davis spoke out to defend the man he called 'a fighter' and claimed that Gascoigne had been put under 'unnecessary pressure' on and off the pitch.

But, of course, Gascoigne is not unique in being a footballer with a drink problem. The list of those who have had to face up to their alcoholism includes some very big names, former England internationals Jimmy Greaves, Malcolm Macdonald, Paul Merson and Tony Adams among them.

Although Gascoigne confesses to being aware he had a possible drink problem as early as 1990, it only came into the public domain eight years later when it was revealed he had been admitted to a drying-out clinic. By then, his short marriage to Sheryl was over.

Gascoigne and his generation of footballers came to prominence at a time when huge money was being thrown at the sport. Footballers had been well paid for generations compared to those who followed them, but the advent of Sky

Sports and a surge in popularity among the middle classes created the conditions for a phenomenal rise in earning power. Contracts worth thousands of pounds a week were suddenly being handed out, yet apart from a few hours of training every day there was often little to fill time.

As Gascoigne demonstrated, the combination of excessive wealth and boredom can be a dangerous mix. He had gone through so much emotionally and physically on his way to Kettering that, when you throw in the pressure he put himself under with all his big promises, it is little wonder he found it all too much.

Some of those who knew and cared for him spoke out. Brian Laudrup, who had been a teammate in that all-conquering Glasgow Rangers team of the 1990s, urged Gascoigne not to follow the destructive path of George Best. 'I think everyone felt when he became the manager of Kettering that Paul was getting his life in order,' he commented. 'Then I heard he had been sacked and feared the worst. When I talk about Paul I can't help but think of George Best and what happened to him. It would be tragic if young people only knew him as someone who attracts bad headlines.'

On the day after Gascoigne's dismissal, both the Football Association and Professional Footballers' Association said they would do what they could to help. Brian Barwick, the FA chief executive, said his organisation would help him gain his coaching badges if that's what he wanted.

Gordon Taylor, the PFA chief executive, said, 'It's a pity the way things worked out at Kettering. It may be back to square one. If a former player has problems he can come to us. But it is down to the person themselves. You can only really provide help when it is asked for.'

Somebody else ready to give an opinion on Gascoigne was Richard Madeley. With his wife, Judy Finnigan, the chat show host had compered the British Book Awards six months prior to Gascoigne's arrival at Kettering. Gascoigne had picked up the prize for sports book of the year and during his time at Kettering appeared on television with the couple. He had come across as perfectly sober. As the war of words raged between Gascoigne and Ladak early that December, Derek Waugh answered the telephone at the *Evening Telegraph* to find Madeley posing the questions. He wanted to know if anybody on the paper had seen Gascoigne drinking alcohol or had any proof that he had been drunk. Waugh told him he had met Gascoigne a couple of times and had twice seen Gascoigne accept a drink from fans, including a bottle of Newcastle Brown. He didn't finish either. But he wasn't the best man to ask as others on the desk had spent more time with Gascoigne and they weren't currently in the office. A few days later, Madeley told readers of his national newspaper column that the local paper had given Gascoigne the all-clear as far as being drunk was concerned.

Madeley had obviously made an impression on Gascoigne, who a few years later revealed how he had turned to the TV chat show host after being sectioned under the Mental Health Act. Gascoigne said he would ring Madeley at 3am, as well as send him texts, because he felt 'so lonely inside' and he knew Madeley would listen. 'When you called back, I didn't take the call but at least I knew you cared for us,' Gascoigne later told Madeley.

A few days after his sacking, another national newspaper quoted a member of the *Evening Telegraph* sports desk as saying Gascoigne was 'always off his face when I saw him, even in press conferences,' but didn't attribute the quote and nobody claimed it. I am confident that nobody on the desk said that. Quite apart from anything else, it simply wasn't true.

Back at Alfreton, Kevin Wilson took a few moments out

from getting his team's attention focused on the game to speak to the media. He did a short piece with BBC Radio Northampton that added little to what was already known and then ran into the wall of journalists chasing yet more quotes about Gascoigne. It was now just over 30 minutes until kick-off and Wilson was keen to get into the dressing room. He said no more than he could get away with without appearing rude.

By the end of a drab 1–1 draw, in which Kettering again conceded a late goal to cancel out their own effort from the recalled Christian Moore, the Gascoigne saga already seemed to be running out of steam. Although a clutch of journalists headed for the dressing room to see if they could squeeze a few more details out of Gascoigne's former players, the demand for Wilson had diminished to the extent that I was able to interview him on my own. I had stood outside the away dressing room listening to him rip into the players, screaming at them that Gascoigne had gone, he wasn't coming back and they had better get used to that right now. Anybody who didn't like it could clear off. The response was total silence.

It had been a difficult 48 hours for Wilson. A couple of the senior players had telephoned him when they heard he had been approached and advised him not to come back. They said the group he was inheriting from Gascoigne was nothing like the one he had handed over less than six weeks previously, specifically in terms of attitude and unity.

Wilson had sensed the shift in attitudes at his first meeting, and speaking to me he was keen to stress that it would not just be a matter of picking up where he had left off: 'Don't go thinking that I'm going to wave a magic wand and it's all going to fall in place. The players have got different habits and you can see that. They still want to play football when people are closing them down but you're not going to win football matches in Conference North playing pretty football week-in, week-out.'

I asked him what he felt of the job done by Gascoigne, and he answered pointedly, 'I'm not really worried about Paul Gascoigne and I'm sure when Paul took the job here he wasn't worried about Kevin Wilson. He was here to do a job, and I get paid by Kettering Town to do a job. My teams are going to play in a different way to that of Paul Gascoigne and Paul Davis.'

Already the Gascoigne era was being consigned to the dustbin of the club's 133-year history. The overhaul continued over the next few days. Ladak announced a freeze on the plan to take the playing squad full-time, although the reserve team was to continue. Only one other club in that division, Northwich Victoria, had a fully professional playing staff, and Wilson had told Ladak he didn't support the idea. With the majority of the squad still doing their day jobs, the players on full-time contracts were to continue with the plan to train with MK Dons. However, the quartet who had been signed under Gascoigne were questioning their positions, and it wasn't long before they started to drift away.

Wilson saw the new signings as a root cause of division in the camp. He felt that whoever signed them had no understanding of the standard they were being brought into, and the money they were being paid had caused seething resentment in some quarters. 'The players they were bringing in might have been good enough to play in Arsenal's reserves or Newcastle's reserves but they weren't good enough to play at this level because they hadn't played in Northern Conference. It was a culture shock to them,' he claimed.

Having run a tight ship under Peter Mallinger, in which the wage bill had been cut year on year, Wilson had been stunned to discover the amount of money that had been thrown at the new players: 'The top players were on £200 to £250 a week, £300 absolute tops, when I left. Then I went back and found players on £500 a week with long-term contracts. And they weren't what was needed. Ryan-Zico Black had done very well in a poor side at Lancaster, he was a decent player and a lovely bloke, but the squad didn't need him.'

The money and drama of the Gascoigne era had unsettled players Wilson had found willing disciples of his work ethic only a short while previously. 'The day after I got approached about returning, I got phone calls from a couple of players I trusted. They said, "Don't do it, don't come back, they're not the same players you brought into the club, their heads have been turned."'

The draw at Alfreton had kept Kettering in sixth place, and there was still hope that a challenge for promotion could be mounted, even if the more realistic target was the end-of-season play-offs. Wilson decided that for the forthcoming Saturday trip to Workington he would take the squad up on the Friday evening for an overnight bonding session.

For Workington, news of Gascoigne's dismissal had been a bitter blow, and threatened to leave them out of pocket. As with the clubs Kettering had visited with Gascoigne as manager, great excitement had been generated by the prospect of seeing the England legend on their turf. Attendances were trebled or more when Gascoigne hit town, and for clubs at this level it produced welcome additional income.

Workington had enjoyed a big increase in the advanced sales of tickets for the game. They had also landed some sponsorship on the back of Gascoigne's anticipated appearance at Borough Park. Now they were so concerned about having to hand the money back that I took a call from them asking if there was any possibility that Gascoigne would be turning up of his own accord, and, if not, whether

I could give them a contact number so they could invite him as their special guest.

Gascoigne's impact on the Conference North had been immense. Whatever the problems at Kettering, he had raised the profile of the club and the league enormously. Lancaster Town were immediately linked with a move to offer him a role at their club, and anyone who wanted a bit of cheap publicity could ensure a couple of column inches by throwing Gascoigne's name into the hat.

Despite everything that had gone wrong at Kettering, there were still many who saw the potential in Gascoigne to make money for themselves. He could bring people through the turnstiles, grab the attention of sponsors and pretty much guarantee that anybody who crossed his path could enjoy their 15 minutes of fame. Shortly before he had been appointed manager at Kettering, he had complained about people wanting to make money out of his name. The wheel just kept on turning.

13

BREAKING DOWN...
IN GAZZA'S
OWN WORDS

THE MOMENT when everybody outside Kettering saw for themselves quite how badly Gascoigne had been affected by the trauma of his sacking came when he gave an interview to Sky Sports News. It was on the Monday evening a few hours after the dismissal had been made public.

Whatever the press had written, and there were thousands and thousands of words printed about Gascoigne over those few days, for the country at large it was his 14-minute interview with Sky that painted the clearest picture of his downfall.

The interview was conducted during the charity event in Liverpool, and the only real talking point was his sacking. His agent, Jane Morgan, tried to persuade him against speaking about Kettering, but Gascoigne still hoped to wrestle the club from Ladak. Under the influence of prescription drugs and alcohol, he was prepared to at least try to answer all the questions put to him.

'People watching that interview were seeing what we'd seen for a long time,' says Brett Solkhon. 'The players all knew how bad he'd been the night before and how much it had hurt him to get sacked. He did need to be sacked. There are two sides to him but he's had plenty of chances to help himself and he always goes back to the drink.'

It was an interview which seemed to polarise opinion among the viewing public: many were horrified to see Gascoigne stuttering and stumbling throughout, clearly distressed and often repeating and contradicting himself. They were saddened and sympathetic. Forget the football, this was a man in need of help.

However, there were those who turned on Gascoigne, accusing him of inflicting all the suffering on himself. In an age of the internet message board, when people can hide behind pseudonyms and dish out abuse with no comeback, some seemed to delight in insulting him.

Here is the transcript of that interview. It makes uncomfortable reading, and reveals quite how bad things were for Gascoigne at that time.

Sky: How's today unfolded for you? Can you tell us when you first heard there were problems today?
PG: I didn't hear it, I knew. I spoke to the chairman after the game. He tried to pick the team. I wouldn't let him. He tried to get players in, tried to get players out, I wouldn't let him. As far as I was concerned, I was the manager and my assistant, a great assistant, was Paul Davis. He questioned both of us, what team I selected. At the end of the day, I'm the manager, I select the team, that's it. I'm emotional, I'm upset, I've been let down. He's making excuses, there's no excuse. He wanted his team and I rejected his team, what he wanted to play. I played my team. So he questioned me after the game when we got beat. I've lost two games in nine games, I've lost twice in nine games, imagine if I'd lost two games in a row. I stuck by my players and my players

have rung me up and they are behind me, Kettering's behind me, the staff is behind me, everyone's behind me. Unfortunately the thing is the chairman's not.

Sky: So were do you go from here?
PG: Where do I go?

Sky: Where do you go from here?
PG: Where I go from here is that as far as I'm concerned I'm not sacked because I never signed a contract. So you can't sack someone who hasn't signed a contract. And I've paid my own way and I paid the staff and I paid everybody else at the club. Where I go from here is I'm going to continue with my director of football Andy Billingham and my financial adviser to buy Kettering Football Club. So I will make Andy Billingham the chairman and I will continue to be the manager and bring the team and club forward the way it should be.

Sky: But the current chairman says he won't sell.
PG: He won't sell? Well, it's a battle there. As we spoke, and I'll tell you the truth, I've got nothing to hide, there's a battle ... there's a battle that the chairman, who is a doctor, and I am Paul Gascoigne the footballer. He's told me he's been watching football for five years, watching football for 20 years, five games a week, and knows how football should be played. Well, the guy can't trap a bag of cement as far as I'm concerned.

Sky: Where does this all leave the players and the fans? They must be very, very confused tonight.
PG: Well, you talk about Brian Clough when he walked away from the team, I ain't walking away. Brian Clough is my idol regards management. Forget about the rest,

Brian Clough ... and I think, no, I'll do it my way and I'm going to do it my way and I'll continue to do it my way. Unfortunately, I know that as a manager you have to stick by the chairman's decisions. His decisions were this team, that team, this team, this player, that player, get rid of him ... no, I stuck by my own guns. I stuck the way I think football should be played. I stuck with, er, I stuck with, erm, I stuck by everything. The staff, everybody, the way the club should be. Even complained about the crowds went to one thousand two hundred and fifty, it was six hundred before I took over so they have risen by six hundred, he's complaining about that.

Sky: He says the players have been played out of position, he says they are confused. What support have you had from the players?
PG: They're confused? They're confused because he come in and told the players that I'll be giving you contracts, professional contracts, and then 10 days later he's wanting me to get rid of them. Two players in my team have just been called up by England foot ... England FA to play for them. He doesn't want to sign one of them and the other one – I won't go into that 'cos that's terrible what he said. I won't go into that.

Sky: What's going to happen with the next game at Alfreton? There's been people wondering whether you are going to take training. You've said that perhaps you might be getting on the coach.
PG: I'm sacked but I'm turning up. I'm sacked but I'm turning up. I am sacked from ... well, I'm not sacked, at the end of the day I own the club, I run the club, I don't own it but I still do, regardless. I said I would never walk away from the next club I take on, I won't walk away.

Sky: So what's going to happen tomorrow when you try and get on the coach and they've already put Kevin Wilson back in charge?

PG: No problem ... no problem. Get the security men there. I ... if not, I get in the car but I tell you what, me, Paul Davis, Andy Billingham are still going to go there. And if not I'm going to meet the players and I'll go behind the dug-out and I'll give instructions from the dug-out, behind the dug-out and still instruct my players how to play and how not to play 'cos they respond to me than the next manager, 'cos that's what they've done, they responded to me. I've had all the players on to me since one o'clock this morning, at night, I've not slept. I spoke to them all, they are all behind me. The players are behind me, the staff is behind me, Kettering Town is behind me, everyone is behind me. The only one who is not behind me is the chairman because I will not play his team. He's a control freak, and that's it.

Sky: What do you make of his accusation that you've not been able to carry out your duties properly? He's gone on to say...

PG: He's saying drink, yeah, he's saying drink. Listen, I've stuck by my job for five or six weeks, I've done well, I'm going through a tough time, it's not a problem. I've had ... counsel, I'm doing a new book. Yeah, I've said since I broke my neck, nearly broke my neck, I've had tough times in my life. This last year's been tough, regardless of my ex-wife, my ex-kids, everything. Everything I've had to deal with. George Best was a personal friend of mine, a personal friend. I lost a good friend and I had his son, Calum Best, called me and I told him, next to his dad, we both loved each other 'cos we both know where we're coming from, me and George Best, regards getting hassled by the press. So what, I had a double brandy. I'll tell you the truth, yeah, I had a double brandy before the game. Before it used to be four bottles of whisky. It's not anymore. I had a double brandy before the game and that was it. I was in a right fit state, I spoke to Paul Davis, who's been at Arsenal for 20-odd years, yeah, I was fine. I spoke to Chris Waddle who I was sitting next to at the game, I was fine. I spoke to Andy Billingham, I was fine. I spoke to players, was I fine? Yes. I'm starting to question myself now, am I good enough to be a manager? Why should I be doing that because of a doctor? I tell you what, yeah, you'll find this week I've not had a drink. I'm not interested in a drink. I had a drink after the game with Paul and Andy, a glass of wine that I didn't even drink anyway. I had a mouthful and that was it because I wanted to concentrate on the team. And then I went to the chairman and said, 'Listen, don't get involved with my job, my job is the manager. I pick the players, I tell who's coming in, who's not coming in. I am the manager.'

Sky: So when he talks about more than 30 incidents over the eight-week period involving alcohol you'd reject that totally?

PG (sneers): Ask the staff. Ask the staff. There's a guy there called Sid, he's been at the club for 50-odd years. The chairman sacked him. I reinstated him. I brought him back in. The next day. Why did he sack … why did he sack Sid? Sid is, Sid is … why did he sack him? I brought him in and I paid these from me own pocket. I paid the groundsmen, I paid Sid, I paid the, er, kitman out of my own pocket. I've not been paid. I do everything for the players, I'm doing everything I can to move Kettering forward and he's moving them backwards, that's what I'm saying.

Sky: So where does the club go from here?

PG: Well, hopefully with a bit of luck, forward. But it won't be going forward until I get back. I will go back.

Sky: And your message to the chairman would be what then?

PG: He's not a chairman [laughs] ... he's not. He's Imraan the doctor. Forget about the next whoever, I'm Paul Gascoigne and I take charge of this club. The club is mine and I love the fans and I love the players and the players are behind me. So regards what they're saying, excuses, drink, this, whatever, me, Paul Davis and Andy Billingham have took this club forward so much it's unbelievable, and I met fans that are behind me. Next week I've got to talk in front of 200 people, now it's over a thousand. They are all behind me. Where do we go? I don't know.

Sky: You seem so determined to carry on and ...

PG: Yeah, I am ...

Sky: You've got so much money invested now, you can't afford to turn round, can you?

PG: I'm a millionaire, a multi-millionaire and I'm angry, yeah. And I will ... I tried to buy him out today and he's said there's not enough money in the world will buy him out. Well, I've told him one on one. The fans against Paul Gascoigne or a doctor, let's see who wins. I hope he's a good doctor. Because Paul Gascoigne will win.

Sky: The fans might start to worry about the future of the club if they've got two people so deeply opposed to each other ...

PG: No they won't. 'Cos there's either going to be me in the club or him, that's it. So, if I leave, that depends on the fans. If the fans want me out, I'll leave and with my hands up like a man, like a proper man. Not making excuses. Like a proper man. I won't make excuses, I'll leave and hold my hands up and say I didn't do my job properly, which I know I did. Or they can have him, a doctor, in charge. And yeah, he'll bring Kevin Wilson back to back himself up, he's got no back-up. All I will do is stick by my guns and go against the chairman. Not many managers do. I have. I went against the chairman, his decisions, his team, and everyone ... he's brought in players that are not good enough for me. I brought in players that are.

Sky: How interesting is it going to be on that team coach then tomorrow?

PG: Er, I tell you what the dressing room will be. There's going to be 18 players that are behind Paul Gascoigne and not Imraan, and I stress Imraan not the chairman. Imraan. Maybe I've lost my job for life regards all chairmans in this country who own top clubs. But [shrugs shoulders] unfortunately I stick by my guns. I stick by my guns and I will not let a chairman tell me how to pick my team.

Sky: Do you regret ever getting involved at Kettering?

PG: No, I love Kettering. I love the fans. I love everybody involved in Kettering. And if that was the case I wouldn't be trying to buy a house in Kettering today. And if that were the case I wouldn't be asking to get £100,000 out of the bank today to buy shares in this club so I have a part in this club.

Sky: So, regardless of what he says, you're so determined to carry on this path and you're so determined to still buy the club out, and you're convinced that ...

PG: No I'm not going to buy the club out, I'm going to buy him out ...

Sky: ... buy him out, but you're also convinced that you've got the support of the fans and the players.

PG: I've got it. And the players. And my staff. I've got everyone ... the players, the staff, the supporters. He wants to do it his way, he wants to make up allegations, he wants to make up the lies, let him do it. The fact is, I'll tell you the fact [pointing] and yous who are listening [points at camera], the fact is I would not pick his team. He's a control freak and that's it, and that's letting everyone know. And I'll tell you one thing, I will not pick his team. I'll stick by my team and I'll stick with my guns and I've had the PFA, I've had the FA, I've had everyone on my side. I'm doing the right thing. If that's not enough for everybody, I don't know what is, but I tell you what, yeah, two years ago I would have give in, I would have give in two years ago, but now I'm stronger and I'm the man, I'm a genius and I know what goes on on the football field. I've made my players better players. Two of my players have been just called up for England, two of my players are wanted by top teams all because of Paul Davis, not me, Paul Davis who I brought in. I'm just the manager, I have the dirty work to do, not to bring in, who not to bring in and do the sad things, you're dropped, and all, that's my job. Which is hard but I do it. But I still hug them and kiss my players. I still fucking care for this club. That's how much hurt I am. It's hurt me badly. And I've been stitched up by a doctor, that's all. So I'm telling you now [looking at camera], Kettering fans, you have Imraan or you have me. Don't worry, I'll still be there tomorrow, I'll be supporting you, whether it's in the crowd, behind the crowd, in the dug-out, I'll still be there. But there's only going to be one winner. Me. Whether I'm still at the club or not, at least I walked away with my head held high and proud. I am proud. And I'll tell you what, a sad day ... [starts to break down] that's how bad I am ...

14

MOORE'S NOT THE MERRIER

CHRISTIAN MOORE surprised himself that he outlasted Paul Gascoigne at Rockingham Road. The pair had fallen out as the dressing room disintegrated and Moore knew it was only a matter of time before he was on his way.

He had arrived at Kettering three months ahead of Gascoigne. A striker, 32 years old at the time and with widespread experience of the non-League game, he enjoyed three spells at Burton Albion, scoring 71 goals in 145 starts. He had been managed by Nigel Clough, who he greatly admired, and, in a 13-year senior career, had earned many friends.

A tenacious character popular with teammates and fans alike, he had been told towards the end of November that he was no longer wanted at Kettering and ordered to stay away.

It wasn't the fact that he was being shown the door that got to him, as he had half-expected that, having exchanged words with Gascoigne after the disappointing draw at Vauxhall Motors. What really got to him was the way in which Gascoigne got Andy Billingham to leave a message on his answerphone. It told him he was being let go and not to turn up for training any more. That so rankled with Moore that he jumped into his car and drove from his Derby home to Kettering to confront Gascoigne.

Moore normally shared a car with three other players to and from training in a bid to save money. As they became increasingly rattled by events at Rockingham Road, the best way that he, Wayne Diuk, Jamie Paterson and Hugh McAuley could cope was by trying to make a joke of it all. The car was often filled with laughter on the way back from training or a match as they recounted Gascoigne's latest antics. But on the day he received Billingham's answerphone message he was far from amused, as he drove the 70 miles to Kettering on his own.

Like most of the other players, Moore had started that season with hopes of a challenge for promotion from Conference North. Having joined on a 12-month contract during the summer, he had fitted in quickly with Wilson and his teammates, and felt they were heading in the right direction. He'd been in the game long enough to have lived through false dawns, and was more wary than excited when he first heard of the takeover plans. But he had admired Gascoigne the footballer and wanted to see how events unfolded. It didn't take long for disillusionment to set in.

Wilson had signed Moore because of his reputation at this level. He was a hard-working and gutsy goalscorer who had spent most of the previous season out because of a knee ligament injury. He kicked off his Kettering career with two goals on his debut and was regularly finding the net in early autumn, although he was coming back from suspension when Gascoigne and Davis took charge of their first game. He was a player with few frills, but his teammates loved him for the way he worked his socks off for the side, never gave up a cause as lost, battered defenders and had a decent scoring record. With his big heart, he was just the sort of player you needed when things weren't going well.

He had been named on the bench for the new manager's first game, and scored the first goal of the Gascoigne era in the 1–0 victory over Droylsden after coming on as a second-half substitute. He had earned a kiss on the cheek from Gascoigne in the dressing room afterwards. Although he found it absurd at training three days later to be told he had to start playing like Zidane, he enjoyed the pizzas when training was over.

Despite being a man who naturally shies away from the spotlight, he was prepared to give Gascoigne a chance. He certainly didn't want any part of the media attention now focused on the club. He found himself in and out of the team and got the feeling his face didn't fit. As someone who simply wanted to play football, he found much of what happened in that period so bizarre that he frequently uses the word 'circus'.

He found training under Paul Davis a chore, and felt that the coach and his manager had little idea what was needed at a level of the game they were unfamiliar with. He grew increasingly frustrated by the insistence on defenders having to pass the ball among themselves until it was given away. So when he was criticised by Gascoigne after the draw at bottom club Vauxhall Motors, where Poppies were lucky to escape with a point against opponents who played a large part of the game with 10 men, it was time to speak up.

'By this stage it was one of the worst changing rooms I had been in,' reveals Moore. 'It was a complete mess. At the start of the season I was happy there, and thought we had a chance of going up. I thought Kettering were putting a decent team together. I scored twice on my debut against a former club, Worcester City, and was looking forward to the rest of the season.'

Moore felt the takeover was handled badly as far as the

players were concerned, with nobody taking time to explain how the relationship between Gascoigne, Davis and Wilson was expected to work. He felt Wilson had been 'stitched up' by being told he was to be director of football when the duties as deemed by Gascoigne clearly didn't fit the job title, and he was disappointed when the former manager left the club.

He wondered exactly what was going to happen when he heard the likes of Les Ferdinand and Teddy Sheringham being linked with the club. He was concerned that what they had achieved could be undermined by PR stunts and headline-grabbing speculation, and was further baffled by the way in which talks over the proposed move to a full-time squad were handled.

'I had a loyalty to Kevin because he had signed me, but when your manager leaves you just have to get on with it, it's out of your hands,' says Moore, who had a day job in insurance. 'I think that's the way a lot of the lads thought, we couldn't influence any of it.

'There was talk of the club going full-time, and I didn't know how it was going to affect me. People had got jobs, and what were they expected to do? I had signed a year's contract on part-time but I would have considered going full-time if the money was right. I was 32, with commitments, and for me it was purely about the money. I lived in Derby and would have to travel into Kettering every day. To give up a full-time job it had to be worth it.'

While teenager Andy Hall was offered a full-time contract almost immediately, senior players were made to wait. 'We had to fill in a form after a midweek game saying what we'd expect to be getting as a full-time player,' recalls Moore. 'I told them what I'd want.'

Moore, already one of the better-paid players, asked for between £750 and £800 a week. 'Bearing in mind what I was earning already and I had a full-time job, plus travelling, that wasn't unreasonable. I never heard a word,' he says.

Keen to enjoy his football, Moore got his head down and tried to concentrate on his own game, but found that increasingly difficult as the new style of play left the forwards starved of the ball. It came to a head at Vauxhall Motors.

'By then everyone knew the way we were playing was wrong, but what do you do?' Moore reflects. 'Most of the players had had enough. Before that game I don't think anyone challenged the team selection, but there was lots of talk among the players about people playing out of position and the style of play. You could see it in the results. We were dropping down the table and looked like we were just going to drop and drop.'

Moore, given only scraps to feed on, was hauled off after 66 minutes, and exchanged words with Gascoigne in the dressing room. 'I asked him why he had taken me off,' he remembers. 'He mumbled something about I hadn't held the ball up, but that was rubbish because I hadn't been given the ball. By that time I really didn't want to be there and thought I was going to have my say. I was a 32-year-old bloke, I had earned the right to say what I thought, and I told him, "If you can get a video of the game I'll go through it with you and we'll see how many times I gave the ball away." I hadn't given the ball away because I hadn't had it. I told him, "All we do is pass it across the back four, it never comes forward." A couple of the other lads chipped in with what they thought and he walked out.'

Gascoigne was also to walk out on Moore a few days later after trying to drive him out of the club. 'Paul had his PR guy, Andy Billingham, around all the time,' recalls Moore. 'After the first game, I had to do a press interview because I had scored and he came up to me and was saying to me, "Be positive about Gazza, be positive about this, be positive about that." I was thinking, "It's like being in the West End yet this is non-League football." I didn't like all that.'

Billingham telephoned Moore on the Thursday following the Vauxhall Motors game. 'I was at work and he left a message on my phone saying there's a couple of clubs in for me, Ilkeston Town, a local team for me with Nigel Jemson the manager, and Cambridge United. He said, "Paul thinks you should go and he doesn't want you to come to training again," and that was pretty much it. I rang him back and said, "You tell him I'll be there for training tonight. He isn't treating me like that."'

Moore got into his car and headed to Rockingham Road. 'I walked in and they were not best pleased to see me. I went straight into his office; the manager and chairman were sat in there, so I had it out with him [Gascoigne]. He wouldn't look me in the eye. He listened to what I had to say and then got up and said to Imraan, "You've got to deal with this, I can't deal with this," and he started to walk out of the room.

'I was fuming. You don't try to get rid of a player via some PR bloke. So I told him he was taking the piss and I wasn't accepting it. I didn't care who he was, how big he'd been as a player. All he was now was the manager who tried to ship me out behind my back.

'If he didn't want me then he should be the one to tell me, that's a different matter. But getting some PR bloke to ring me up and say you don't need to come training any more, that's out of order. Fans get to look at that and think, "He's not turning up, he's not bothered." He still didn't say anything, so I told him, "At the end of the day I've lost all respect for you if you can't even answer me."'

As far as Moore was concerned, his time was up. 'I thought I was finished and it was just about waiting for another club to come in. The manager didn't want me and the chairman thought I was going. But I'd been in the game a long time and wasn't going to do anything stupid. I just carried on turning up for training.'

Nothing came of the Ilkeston interest and Moore didn't want to drive to Cambridge three times a week. 'A couple of weeks later, he [Gascoigne] comes up to me and says, "I've been impressed with the way you've trained and you're part of my plans." By then I was not interested in what anybody at that club had to say because it was a circus, it really was a circus. He got sacked a few days later.'

Moore received a tearful phone call from Gascoigne telling him that Ladak was trying to sack him. It was the only time Moore answered his phone to find Gascoigne on the line without going through Davis or Billingham. He told Moore he had rated him as a footballer and it had been Ladak who wanted him out. 'He was crying, saying he had wanted to keep me, it was Imraan who wanted rid of me, that he was being stitched up,' Moore claims. 'I got my wife to listen in with me. This was a guy I had worshipped as a player, and here he was crying down the phone to a bloke who his PR guy had told a couple of weeks ago he didn't want at the club. To me, it was a phone call out of desperation, and I felt sorry for him. It was just a sad, sorry state of affairs.'

After Gascoigne's sacking, Ladak told Moore it had been Gascoigne who had wanted him out. By that stage Moore didn't know who to trust. He was one of a number of players who believed one of the new signings had only been taken on because he was a friend of the chairman. 'I thought one player was an insider, a bit of a snitch, and a lot of the players felt the same. The dressing room had completely gone,' he recalls.

When Wilson returned, he told Moore that he was being taken off the transfer list. 'I said no, I really didn't want to be a part of it,' he admits. 'To me, Kevin had been stitched up in the way he originally left the club, then he's appointed a few hours after Paul's been dismissed. There must have been talks going on in that time. There's a lot of bullshitters in football, a lot of people who are a bit underhand. I didn't know who to trust and trust is a big thing at a football club. When I joined, it was Peter Mallinger and Kev. Then it was Imraan and Kev, and I told Kev that part of the reason I didn't want to stay was because of the chairman.

'I had Paul saying it was Imraan's decision for me to leave and then Imraan telling me it was Paul's. Things weren't being run right. OK, Paul had gone and Kev, who I trusted, was back. But the chairman was still there and I didn't want to play for him.'

Moore finally got the move he craved when he returned to Burton Albion for a third time a month later, having found himself dropped down the pecking order following the signing of highly rated striker Anthony Elding from Stevenage. 'I started being left out altogether and then I got the chance to go back to Burton. That was my club, the best club I've played for, the club I loved playing for. For me to leave Kettering, who were Conference North, to go back to the Conference with the team I love, well, I went with a big smile on my face. They didn't have to pay a fee, although I was told they asked Burton for a bag of balls for me. I found that a bit insulting.'

Moore was delighted to be back working at a stable club under Nigel Clough. 'I'd have played for Nigel for next to nothing. When I first heard of Burton coming in for me, I said to Kevin, "You better make this happen. I'm not staying at Kettering." Burton was the club I wanted to play for, and Kevin knew that. I said, "Make sure nothing goes wrong in this deal because if it does I won't be pleasant to have around the club."'

Even as he said his goodbyes to his teammates of six months, Moore was picking up whispers about who was picking the team at Kettering. 'I don't think for one minute Kev would let a chairman pick his team for him, but you were still hearing things,' he recalls. 'By then so much had happened that you could believe almost anything.

'Imraan was a football supporter who ended up running a football club and had plenty to learn. Paul Gascoigne and Paul Davis were from a different level of football completely and they didn't get how a club like Kettering worked. That wasn't their fault, we were just not as good players as they had been. But who brought them to the club?'

15

NO HAPPY RETURN
FOR WILSON

CHRISTIAN MOORE'S insistence on leaving was one of many factors that doomed to failure Kevin Wilson's attempt to pick up the shattered pieces of Paul Gascoigne's era. In a tumultuous season of chop and change, Wilson's second spell as manager lasted only 59 days before he, too, was sacked. On 2 February 2006, he left the club for the second time in three months, feeling even more bitter than he had the first time.

His second coming, in early December, had been warmly greeted by the players who knew him and many of the supporters who craved a sense of stability after all the trauma of the Gascoigne drama. Wilson was the level-headed plain-talker who would quickly restore a sense of normality. He'd sweep away the fancy ideas, the team would go back to basics, there'd be no more distractions and, if anybody saw themselves as a big-time Charlie, well, they'd better watch out.

Ladak, a chairman for less than six weeks, had few contacts in the non-League game. The reappointment of Wilson was logical. With a little bit of luck, he'd pick up where he had left off and the chairman could begin to put Gascoigne behind him.

'It had got to the stage where all we wanted to do was get back to where we were before,' recalls Neil Midgley. 'We'd got through the Gascoigne period, we'd survived, we'd had our three minutes of fame, and now everything was going to be hunky-dory again. The pressure had been piling up over the previous few weeks and suddenly it felt like there was a real weight off our shoulders.'

'I thought it would be business as usual,' adds Diuk.

But it wasn't quite that simple. A hornet's nest had been stirred and Wilson quickly discovered that the divisions within the camp could not be healed as easily as he had hoped: the scars ran deep. The four new players who had signed to be part of the Gascoigne experience were shell-shocked. They had had no chance, or encouragement, to be woven into the fabric of the squad. Others who had not even been certain of starting a game under Wilson in early October were now on long-term contracts. And some longer-serving players resented what they saw as lesser players being paid more than them, with the security of those treasured long-term contracts to boot.

There was suspicion in the dressing room as to who was playing for the chairman, who was playing for the manager, who was still hankering for the bright lights of Paul Gascoigne and who wanted to get away. As Christian Moore says, trust was in short supply.

Wilson had to address all this while also sorting out the tactics and style of play that had caused so much chaos on the pitch. There was also the issue of the half-baked plans to take the squad full-time and what to do about the newly launched reserve team.

Although Ladak had enticed him back with the offer of a three-year contract, Wilson returned on a part-time basis.

That didn't help. He had a handful of full-time players off training with another club at Milton Keynes, some of his senior players were questioning how much influence the chairman was still having on playing matters and the aftershocks of the Gascoigne era were still being felt.

What to do about the Paul Gascoigne fundraising dinner scheduled for 14 December was another distraction. More than 300 tickets had been sold and the club wasn't even in control of a function that was to prompt another ugly public spat.

If Wilson was to turn Kettering's season around, he had to sort the mess out, and quickly. The talk was that the play-offs were still a possibility. And, in accepting Ladak's offer to pick up where he had left off, Wilson felt he'd be able to achieve that goal. He pretty much changed his mind within 15 minutes of walking into the dressing room.

Unfortunately, for himself as much as the club, Wilson returned with a chip on his shoulder. He was bitter and prejudiced, and very disappointed to find all his hard work over the previous couple of years laid to waste.

'After the first game back at Alfreton, I could have walked out that night,' admits Wilson. 'Too many players had changed, too many were in the comfort zone. There had been all this money flying about and I was absolutely astounded when I saw what some of the new players were on. That wasn't up to me. That was up to Paul Gascoigne and Paul Davis and Imraan Ladak, that's how they had dealt with it, but I had to sort that out.

'When Mr Ladak contacted me, I thought I'd get back in there and sort it out. But as soon as I got in there I could see it wasn't going to be a turnaround in two or three weeks, it was going to take months. Players were on ridiculous contracts for this level.

'There was division and I could probably have got rid of

nearly all the squad. The mentality had changed, there wasn't the focus there'd been before. Even the fans had changed because of the Paul Gascoigne thing. Our fans expected us to win every week. Everybody else wanted to do us.'

The initial surge of enthusiasm generated by Wilson's return quickly faded. The new signings felt unwanted, and that was pretty much the truth of their situation. Wilson was having no truck with talk of full-time football, and didn't see how they fitted in. Dixon went almost immediately, returning to the north-east and Seaham Red Star. Fowler, who had earned a decent reputation coming through the ranks at Arsenal, left at his own request a month later to sign for Havant & Waterlooville. Michael McKenzie, born in Milton Keynes and having joined Kettering after spells at Bedford and Raunds, quickly returned to the obscurity of Buckingham Town in the United Counties League. And Ryan-Zico Black was so fed up he gave up two years of his contract to escape.

Although Wilson brought back Jamie Paterson, Moore was on his way out. The manager was determined to strengthen his squad with hungry players who were going to 'wear the shirt with pride'. Kettering paid Stevenage Borough a £40,000 'package' for the highly rated striker Anthony Elding. Then Jermaine Palmer signed on a short-term contract from Hinckley Town, having scored against Wilson's side twice over the festive period.

To help create space for the new strikers, Neil Midgley, a sports science student who had combined his studies in Cambridge with playing on a non-contract basis, was told he was being released. 'I got called into Kev's office and he said, "Sorry, Midge, the chairman says I've got to cut the budget. You're one of the lads on non-contract so we've got to let you go." I was really low, this was my living. I didn't know if it was Kev or Imraan who wanted me out.'

Midgley went back to his former club, Canvey Island, for one training session before Wilson was sacked. Alan Biley, with whom Midgley had a good relationship, returned to Rockingham Road as assistant to new manager Morell Maison. Biley called him up and, seven days after being shown the door, Midgley returned on higher wages than when he had left, and with a contract, in a deal that had been thrashed out at a motorway service station.

In their discussions on the weekend that Gascoigne was sacked, Ladak and Wilson had agreed to scrap plans to take the club full-time. Although that was the beginning of the end for the new signings, some of the longer-serving players were pleased. Club captain Derek Brown was one of those who decided to stay, having looked elsewhere, because, at the age of 31 and with a good job at Argos, he had no intention of packing it in for full-time football on lower wages. 'We are trying to steady the ship now. We are staying part-time and as long as that is the case I want to be part of Kettering Town,' said Brown in mid-December 2005. Just six weeks later he was gone, the first out of the door following Wilson's replacement by the almost unknown Maison.

On his return in early December, Wilson had tried to bully the squad back into shape. It didn't work. 'Too much had been broken,' claims Diuk. 'There was too much to fix. As a side, we were flattened. He'd heard what some of the new players were on and it was too much for him. He just didn't want to pick them. Too many players were unsettled, and any club where the players are unsettled doesn't play well. We had forgotten how to win and when Kev came back he was still bitter from how he had been treated before. He wasn't the same person. He just seemed to blame everything on Gazza, which was true. You'd think 39 days isn't that long but it was, and there had been too much in-fighting. Morale had gone.'

As if Wilson didn't have enough on his plate, he found the chairman paying regular visits to his office to discuss matters he felt were none of his business. Ladak questioned Wilson on team selections and tactics, and why the new signings which he had taken a personal interest in were being bombed out. Wilson was uncomfortable. He put it down to Ladak's enthusiasm but began to understand what had been behind some of Gascoigne's rants.

'A lot of things had changed,' says Wilson. 'All of a sudden I had a chairman who spent more time in my office than he did in the boardroom. When I was there before, Peter Mallinger never came in and talked about the team or about the players, asking why this one isn't playing and why this one is on the bench. It was a rude awakening for me that somebody was coming in and talking about the side when in the past I'd never had that.'

Results were all over the place during Wilson's first few games, with the draw at Alfreton followed by a 3–2 defeat at Workington and two festive draws with Hinckley Town. Kettering went out of the FA Trophy and the only win of his second spell at the club, a 2–0 victory over Lancaster City, came in mid-January. Successive 3–0 defeats to Moor Green and Hyde United saw Ladak sack his second manager in two months. He wasn't sorry to see the abrasive Wilson go.

Ladak was infuriated by a radio interview after the defeat at Hyde in which Wilson said the entire club needed a reality check from top to bottom. It was time for the people running the club to get their heads out of the clouds. 'I've got to be very careful what I say,' Wilson told BBC Radio Northampton. 'But football is just half the problem at the moment.'

'That didn't go down very well so you could say I loaded the gun,' Wilson admits now. 'But I was totally not happy with everything at the club. I found it impossible to replicate the relationship I had with Peter Mallinger. I was disappointed in the players and I was disappointed in myself.

'I was still living in the Paul Gascoigne era. It influenced my thinking and I never really got it out of my head. I am very critical of myself and I didn't do myself any favours when I went back. I know I didn't deal with some of the things very well.

'But I should have been left to do my job and I don't think I was able to do that. I did feel under pressure to put certain players in. Even before he was chairman, when I was manager the first time, he'd come in and say things like, "I like your substitutions." You'd think to yourself, "But that's what I get paid for."'

Although the media coverage of Wilson's dismissal was small fry compared to the many thousands of words written about Gascoigne's departure, there were common threads.

Wilson complained of not receiving a penny in compensation, and felt betrayed. 'I got offered a three-year deal which I accepted on a handshake, and as far as I was concerned that means everything. It was in the papers, on the radio and as far as I am concerned that was it. I never got a penny. I did lose my cool. I wasn't very happy with the man.'

Wilson, a father-of-five, considered chasing Ladak through the courts but decided his family had suffered enough. 'At the end of the day it wasn't about money. It was having a big effect on my family. If you're not careful, these things cost you more than money.'

And if Wilson was no fan of Ladak, it seemed the feeling was reciprocated. Seeing the way in which Gascoigne had cracked up after his sacking had given Ladak a bit of a guilty conscience. Although it had all gone so badly wrong, Ladak had backed Gascoigne and Davis in their attempts to change the style of play. Perhaps he had acted too swiftly, firstly in sacking Gascoigne and then in reappointing Wilson.

'About an hour into the Alfreton game, Kevin turned back to me and said, "This is what the pretty football has done to them [the players],"' Ladak told Jon Dunham in a confessional interview a year later. 'And I thought to myself, "Well, that's the sort of football I want to see."'

He was never going to get that with Wilson. Fearing he had made a hasty decision, Ladak was already reaching for the gun, and, when Wilson's team clocked up successive 3–0 defeats to make it only one win in 12 games, Ladak wasn't slow to pull the trigger. Especially as he had hated the way that Wilson, as he saw it, continued to blame Gascoigne for everything wrong at the club. 'It's about time we forgot about Paul Gascoigne and everything that happened during that spell,' he insisted.

Announcing Wilson's return in early December, Ladak said he had been sad to see Wilson leave the club a month previously. Not this time. In programme notes reflecting on his first three years at Kettering, Ladak said of the time when he sacked Wilson, 'It is impossible to put into context what a mess we were in. The team was in freefall, lacking character, spirit and confidence, and it was difficult to see where a win would come from.'

For the fourth time that season, the players were gearing up for a change of manager. This time Ladak felt he knew exactly what he needed: 'I want an intelligent and articulate manager, but it has to be a purist who will get the team playing the entertaining football everyone wants to see.'

So into the breach stepped Morell Maison. To some, it was more a case of Morell who? 'I had never heard of him,' recalls Diuk. Maison's previous job had been manager of Buckingham Town, several rungs down the ladder. His biggest achievement had been to lead a club which celebrated three-figure crowds to the runners-up spot in the United Counties League premier division in 2004.

Ladak had originally asked him to take charge of the newly formed reserves. Instead, Maison was given the first team, initially as temporary manager. 'I had to deal with the jibes from the not-so-pleasant individuals who wanted to continually spell my name wrong or say, "Morell who?"' says Maison. 'But you have to put up with that in the knowledge you can do your job.'

Maison, a giant of a man with a powerful outgoing personality and a winning smile, saw his first responsibility as steadying a ship that had been buffeted by stormy waters for so long it had lost all sense of direction. He was only going to be positive. He brought back Biley. And he made it clear he wanted the club to be full of happy footballers.

He had an immediate impact with Kettering defeating high-flying Northwich Victoria 2–0 to start a mini-revival of three successive wins.

However, a draw with Hucknall was followed by three defeats and the moaning started again. Maison began bringing in his own players. Moses Olaleye, a 22-year-old winger, was the first to sign, following Maison from Buckingham Town. Nathan Koo-Boothe, a 6ft 4ins 20-year-old defender, was next, having left MK Dons. Patrick Peter, a lanky striker from Sudan who was living in Finland, was also signed, while a handful of players, including Hugh McAuley, were released.

Maison boasted that Kettering had signed Peter in the face of interest from clubs in Estonia, but not everybody was impressed. 'The players he was bringing in were just rubbish,' claims Diuk. 'They were coming from the UCL and God knows where.'

Olaleye replaced Ollie Burgess in right midfield, playing in front of Diuk, who was almost drummed out of the club after an on-field bust-up with Peter. 'One game we played

Vauxhall Motors at home, who were bottom of the league and had just had a man sent off,' Diuk recalls. 'They were absolutely hammering us because these two [Olaleye and Peter] kept giving it away. I thought, "I'm not having this, I keep getting done two on one."

'Patrick was flicking the ball up or balancing it on his head, and he just kept giving it away. I said to him, "Hold the ball up, what are you fucking doing?" I gestured to him to hold the ball up. At training on the Tuesday, Alan Biley pulled me to one side and said the chairman and the manager are talking about getting rid of me. They hadn't liked the way I had gestured to Patrick. "Did you know he went home crying?" Alan said. I said, "You're joking!"'

Biley told Diuk they wanted him to apologise to Peter in front of the other players. He went ballistic, but Biley calmed him down and persuaded him to do it. 'All the lads were there at training and I've gone up to him and said, "Hey, Patrick, I didn't mean to make you cry." I held out my hand, he shook it, and I walked off. What a joke.'

Diuk's mood wasn't improved when the next two signings were announced as unknowns from Hitchin Town and the MK Dons training scheme. The club he had served loyally for seven years was changing beyond recognition. He was released at the end of the season after rejecting the chance to turn full-time on wages of £300, and only learned he was no longer wanted when his father rang him to say he'd just read on the internet about his being freed.

Not that Maison's spell could be classified a failure. His reshaped side put together a decent run that took them close to the play-offs and the following season they challenged for the Conference North title for much of the next campaign.

Kettering were two points behind leaders Droylsden with two games to play at the end of 2006/07 when Ladak again astonished onlookers by sacking Maison. He said he had written off hopes of wrestling the title from Droylsden and wanted a new man in for the play-offs.

Maison discovered he had been fired in a phone call from a player who had read about it on the internet. 'Had we been bottom of the league when I was sacked, I would have understood,' he later reflected. 'Going into what turned out to be my final game at Hinckley, we'd won six on the bounce and hadn't lost for 14 matches.'

Ron Atkinson, who had launched his managerial career at Kettering in the early 1970s, had returned to Rockingham Road three months earlier after a career that had seen him at the helm of some of the biggest clubs in the country, including Manchester United, Aston Villa, West Brom and Sheffield Wednesday. He had been appointed as director of football by Ladak, and enjoyed a good relationship with Maison, and he was so upset at the sacking he took Maison to the pub to share three bottles of champagne and exchange war stories. Forty-eight hours later, he walked out on the club.

Ladak turned to Graham Westley, who had wound up Gascoigne in November 2005 while manager of Stevenage. He was given the final two games plus the play-offs. Westley, who had been sacked by Rushden & Diamonds two months earlier, got a point from a goalless draw at Stalybridge and oversaw a home defeat by Alfreton. Poppies drew both play-off matches against Farsley Celtic and were beaten on a penalty shoot-out.

Ladak then made probably the best decision of his short time as chairman by appointing Mark Cooper as manager. Son of the former Leeds United and England full-back Terry Cooper, Mark had spent the previous three years managing Tamworth after a playing career that had seen him run out for a number of Football League clubs, including Exeter City,

Birmingham City and Hartlepool United. He had then settled into non-League as player and manager.

The next season, Kettering romped to the Conference North title by 17 points to finally reclaim their place in the top flight of the non-League game.

16

THE STRANGE CASE OF RYAN-ZICO BLACK

SO MANY people had their hopes raised by the prospect of Paul Gascoigne becoming manager at Kettering Town. Players and supporters couldn't help but be carried away with the excitement generated by his imminent arrival. Although many of the players ended up bitterly disappointed by their experiences, they were still keen to stress that Gascoigne was one of their favourite players of all time, if not *the* favourite.

The reality of his time at Rockingham Road was all the more miserable because this group of footballers had been so excited at the prospect of working with the sort of legend who simply doesn't get involved at their level. For a short spell, they had a brief taste of what life must be like as a Premier League footballer.

One player who thought he had the world at his feet when he signed for Kettering Town on 17 November 2005 was Ryan-Zico Black, whose name clearly reflects the football-mad family he was born into on 4 August 1981. His Irish father, Dessie, had been a huge fan of Celtic and adored

Brazil, and decided to christen his son Zico, with his mum Sue wisely insisting on the addition of Ryan, just in case her son grew up not liking football.

It was soon clear she needn't have worried. Black was kicking a ball around from the moment he staggered to his feet as a toddler, and by the time he was eight years old he was playing in the under-13 team managed by his dad on the island of Guernsey, where the family lived. At 11, Black had a trial with Southampton and impressed enough to be invited to train with the South Coast club for the next three years, during which time he flew back and forth from the Channel Islands. He moved on to Bournemouth, where he signed schoolboy forms, but he was released when the club went into receivership.

A trial spell with Plymouth Argyle was over almost before it had begun, when Black, then 16, badly sprained his ankle ligaments on the first morning. On his recovery, and still desperate to make it, he had a trial with Morecambe, then in the Conference. He was signed on and moved to Lancashire, where he shared digs with five other young hopefuls as part of the club's newly formed academy, and worked his way into the reserve team at Christie Park and the Northern Ireland Under-18 squad.

The future looked even brighter for the young attacking midfield player when he broke into the Morecambe first team. He was promoted to Northern Ireland's Under-21s and got to play against Germany in a game shown live on German TV. There were reports that Black was among a number of Morecambe players being watched by the likes of Liverpool, Blackburn and Manchester City. He got himself an agent, although that ended in a mess when the agent tried to dissuade him from signing a three-year contract offered by Morecambe, a club to whom Black was loyal.

A move to Northwich Victoria, also in the Conference,

ended in disappointment, and, after a year with Glenavon in Northern Ireland, Black moved to Lancaster City, where he was thrilled to agree a £3,500 signing-on fee and free accommodation. But the cheque bounced, the chairman resigned and, with the club in a mess, he had to settle for a £1,000 signing-on fee and a basic wage. It wasn't the last time Black was to find himself sold short.

Now 24, his career was beginning to drift in the way experienced by many in the non-League game. Hopes of a place at a Football League club were beginning to fade after all the early promise, although he could still dream. In the summer of 2005, he helped Guernsey to the final of the World Island Games in the Shetland Islands despite feeling unwell for much of the tournament, having taken antibiotics for an insect bite that caused his arm to balloon. A knee injury in the opening game of the season for Lancaster meant another spell on the sidelines. Although he returned to action with two goals in his first game back, he was told he was going on the transfer list.

Just when he was beginning to wonder where it had all gone wrong, Black received the phone call he believed would change his life. He had watched Gascoigne's takeover press conference on Sky Sports News with his father, who was on a visit to see his son play, and was thrilled to receive a phone call a few days later from teammate Iain Swan telling him that Kettering had shown an interest. Swan had been told of the approach by the club's physio. Black could scarcely believe it, as he telephoned family and friends to tell them his exciting news, but then 'Swanny' rang him back to say, 'Sorry, mate, it was all a wind-up.' But it wasn't.

With critically poor timing, Black injured a hamstring in his final game for Lancaster, just two days before a fee was agreed with Kettering. He was told he had to set off for Rockingham Road within a couple of hours for a medical, with both Steve Johnston, the Lancaster chairman, and Ladak calling him to stress urgency, and Black was led to believe that Kettering would look to sign another player if he couldn't make it that day.

In a panic, he tried to get hold of his girlfriend, Becky, who was in a lecture at university and had her phone switched off. He eventually picked her up and they set off. He then called Ladak to explain he might be a little late and would probably miss training. 'I didn't want to train anyway as my hamstring wasn't right, and I didn't want to tell them that I was injured in case that put them off,' he recalls. He had no idea of how much money he would be offered but that wasn't his main concern: all he could think of was the prospect of a full-time contract and the chance to play for Gascoigne, whose book he had just finished reading.

He arrived at 8.30pm. The Kettering players were still out training on the pitch, and he headed straight into talks with Ladak. 'I said I wanted £20,000 a year if the club stayed part-time and £25,000 a year when it went full-time,' Black recalled. 'He told me it would be full-time within a month.'

Having agreed a two-and-a-half-year deal, Black thought he'd done well for himself until he learned a few weeks later that another new signing had negotiated a deal worth twice as much. 'I was kicking myself. I should have asked for more but I was too busy thinking what Gazza would be like.'

But first Black would have to undergo a medical, and he was worried he might be pulled up for his tight hamstring but managed to blag his way through. Then came the highlight of the evening as Gazza walked into the physio's room. He gave Black a kiss on the cheek and said, 'Welcome to the new kid on the block.'

By now, the players were tucking into their pizzas. Black was further impressed.

He followed Gascoigne into the manager's office where he

met Paul Davis, and the pair explained to him how they wanted the team to play and how he could be a part of it. He was also ordered not to give interviews without permission. The last thing he was told before he left was that he was in the squad for Saturday's game. He drove Becky to the Kettering Park Hotel, where Ladak had booked them in for the night, and ordered champagne and a meal. 'This was the chance I'd been waiting for,' he says.

He returned to Lancaster the next day and, with his future seemingly secure, went out and bought a Renault Clio. He drove it to Liverpool to meet his new teammates at a hotel ahead of the game against Vauxhall Motors. 'The management talked everything through before the game with Paul Davis doing most of the talking and Gazza saying a few bits after him. My first impression was everything was very professional. I was named on the bench but I was kind of hoping not to play because my hamstring was still not right.'

With 20 minutes remaining of the 1–1 draw, he was sent on. He felt it was good to be part of a side that was at least trying to pass the ball to each other, even if it didn't always work. But he clearly wasn't 100 per cent fit. 'I was limping when I got back from the game and iced it as soon as I got home. I didn't want them to know I was struggling.'

The injury was to be a recurring problem. Although Black came off the bench at half-time for the bitterly disappointing defeat at Redditch three days after his debut, he had to miss training two days later after confessing to the injury. By now the wheels were starting to come off the Poppies' bandwagon in more ways than one, and even the team coach broke down on its way out of Redditch's Valley Stadium. Black reclaimed his car from the M6 services at Corley when the club secretary at Redditch gave him a lift.

With his injury in the open, Black was kept on the bench as emergency cover for the FA Trophy win over

Gainsborough Trinity. The novelty of playing for Gascoigne was still fresh, but he soon picked up on the tension both inside the squad and between manager and chairman, and he quickly became a pawn in the in-fighting.

He had missed the training session ahead of the Trinity game to receive treatment on the troublesome hamstring, but, during the following Tuesday's session, involving first team and reserves, his instincts told him something was wrong. 'I could sense that Paul Davis was being a bit funny with me and that was made clear when he read out the whole first-team squad apart from me to do some drills. That really annoyed me but I just got on with training. I knew something was going on, though, and I started to wonder who wanted me there. There was tension between Gazza and the chairman.'

Unknown to Black, Ladak had been instrumental in taking him to Rockingham Road, as Gascoigne hadn't seen him play and had agreed to the signing on the basis of the chairman's recommendation. Ladak had spoken enthusiastically of the new signing, saying, 'Ryan is already a very good player for this level, but with his confidence and attitude, combined with the style of football we are trying to play, we are confident he can maximise his potential under Paul Gascoigne and Paul Davis.'

And it was clear to senior players that Black had been brought to the club by Ladak, not Gascoigne, something Kevin Wilson acknowledged when he returned to the club after Gascoigne's sacking. 'He was the chairman's signing,' was his blunt assessment.

The players were also questioning how much more Black was being paid than them. With Black not playing to his potential as he tried to camouflage his injury, they weren't impressed.

'They brought Zico in and Christian Moore got dropped,'

says Diuk. 'He was the top goalscorer and we just thought, "This isn't right." We had our two best players on the bench and we weren't sure about Zico. Later on he proved what a good player and lad he was, but at the time I think he admits he wasn't doing too well. And we were becoming bogged down by everything that was happening. It wasn't a good time to be joining.'

Black moved into the George Hotel in Kettering and made use of the local LA Fitness gym. Apart from Andy Hall, Black was the only other player on a full-time contract, and he only met the rest of the squad on match days and for evening training, so bonding with his suspicious new teammates was no easy task.

'I felt sorry for him,' says Moore. 'He'd been brought in by the chairman and all of a sudden there were two different managers. I don't think anyone thought anything against him. He was a nice lad, but there were rumours he was on a lot of money on a three-year contract and that rankled with some of the lads.'

Gascoigne told Black he wanted him to commit to the club by moving to the area, so he started to look at houses and flats to rent, but, before he found one, Gascoigne was gone.

Two days after a 3–1 home league defeat by lowly Barrow, Black received a phone call telling him to get to Kettering for a team meeting that evening. The first he knew of Gascoigne's sacking was when he heard about it on his car radio.

The Barrow defeat had been the final straw for Ladak. Black had not made the squad for that match, but he was shocked and saddened by Gascoigne's departure. 'I was gutted. He was the reason I signed in the first place and had committed to a long-term contract.'

Three other players had joined Black at Kettering. Kevin Dixon, Michael McKenzie and Jordan Fowler were still learning the names of their new colleagues when Gascoigne was sacked. 'The players that Gazza had brought in were disappointed he had gone but not everyone was sad, especially when Kev Wilson came back. This was his squad before Gazza took over.'

Black claims he quickly realised that he was going to have a problem with Wilson: 'I knew I wouldn't be his type of player.'

After his first training session under Wilson on the Monday evening, Black went off to find Ladak to discuss his position. 'He was too busy having a slanging match with Paul Gascoigne live on Sky Sports News.' So Black got himself a Coca-Cola and sat down to watch Ladak, then Wilson, talking on TV about what was happening all around him.

Black hoped his Northern Ireland connection might stand him in good stead with Wilson, but found himself dumped in the reserves after one game as an unused substitute. 'He told us, "All this playing out from the back and fancy football stops now. We are going to become hard to beat again, start grinding out some results and climb the league."'

Wilson also told them he was ending Gascoigne's plan to take the squad full-time.

With a cull of Gascoigne's signings in the offing, Black feared that, by virtue of his two-and-a-half-year contract, he was going to be left to rot. Wilson, always straight, told Black he felt his best position was as part of a three-man forward line but, as a manager, he never played with three upfront. 'In fairness to Kev, he always told me to my face what he thought and you can't ask for much more than that, even if it was negative things he was saying. I wish more managers would do the same instead of just telling you what you want to hear,' he said.

All this was a far cry from the excitement Black had felt

three weeks earlier, when he had driven down from Lancaster with his heart thumping at the prospect of signing for Gascoigne. During his first conversation with the England legend, he was like a star-struck schoolboy, hanging on Gascoigne's every word. 'He said to me, "I'm no longer Gazza the football legend, well I'll always be that, but now I'm your gaffer, the boss, that's all. Believe in yourself and every time you go on the pitch believe that you are the best player – have that in your head every game you play. When I was playing, I thought I was better than Pele, Best, Maradona. I probably wasn't, but I honestly believed I was when I was on the pitch."'

There were to be few good moments for Black over the coming months. Although he respected Wilson for having the guts to tell him to his face he didn't fit in, Ladak encouraged him to work hard, and said he still wanted him to find a home in Kettering. He also told him he wanted him to go training with MK Dons.

By now, Black had moved out of the hotel and was living back in Lancaster, only driving down when required. 'I didn't want to commit to moving until I started playing regularly. Kev Dixon left as he was getting messed about and Jordan was thinking of leaving, while Michael McKenzie wasn't getting a look-in. I talked to Jordan about the Dons training and he didn't fancy it either. I was getting down about football, my confidence was low and I lost interest in training. It was a long way to go just to train and even if we did train it wouldn't mean we would get a game at Kettering.'

With Wilson determined to erase all traces of the Gascoigne era as quickly as possible, Black thought the game was up when he arrived at Rockingham Road for the Boxing Day fixture against Hinckley United. He was five minutes late and was left out of the squad.

He walked out of the stadium and spent most of the game in a town-centre Subway before returning. 'I asked Kev why he wasn't giving me a chance and told him I'd leave if he wanted, but that I'd want paying up. He said no chance. I asked if I could go on loan and he didn't want me doing that either. I was getting sick of the driving and thought if I could go on loan somewhere up north I could get the same money, with Kettering paying half and my loan club paying the rest, and I'd save on all the petrol.'

As he drove away from the ground in a dark mood, Black stopped at a service station and rang the Barrow manager Phil Wilson. He told him he could join them as long as there wasn't a fee to be paid. However, Wilson told Black that Ladak wasn't going to let him leave without getting back at least some of the £10,000 they had paid for him. Black didn't travel for the return game at Hinckley on 2 January, and phoned Wilson to tell him he was sick. Wilson told him to send in a doctor's note.

Black couldn't see any way back. Then along came Garry Thompson. A respected striker, he had played for the likes of Coventry City, Aston Villa, West Brom and Sheffield Wednesday, and his final club as a player had been Northampton Town, where he was also given some coaching responsibilities by manager Ian Atkins. He left to be replaced by Wilson in 1997 and went on to manage Bristol Rovers.

Thompson was appointed Wilson's second-in-command at Kettering early in January 2006. He liked what he saw in Black and told him he would push the striker's case with Wilson if he worked hard. Within a fortnight, Black was called into the manager's office to be told he would be starting the league game against Lancaster City.

Unable to stay out of trouble for long, Black got it in the neck from the players and supporters of his former club after scoring. Some of his ex-teammates and the local paper in

Lancaster accused him of overdoing the celebration and said he had kissed the badge on his Poppies shirt, something Black fiercely denies. 'Yes, I did celebrate but I definitely didn't kiss the badge. That's one thing that I wouldn't do unless I'd been with a club for years and years,' he claims. 'With all the frustration I'd had for the month before, it was a relief to score and it was unfortunate that it happened to be against Lancaster.'

Although Kettering went on to win that game 2–0, it was the only league win they were to register in Wilson's second spell at the club, which ended in his sacking amid further recriminations between manager and chairman.

Wilson's final game saw Black start on the bench, as the manager changed his formation. With his team trailing 3–0, he threw Black into the fray. Black was singled out for a compliment by Wilson in the dressing room afterwards, but, he reveals, 'That was the first bit of praise I had received since I arrived at the club.'

Black couldn't believe he was saying goodbye to his second manager in little over a month. Having finally convinced Wilson he was worth his place, he was again fretting over whether he'd fit in with the next manager through Ladak's revolving door. Wilson, having gathered his belongings for a second time in three months, popped his head round the door of the treatment room to tell Black his opinion of him had been changed. 'He wished me luck and I did the same,' he said.

For the third time in two months, Black was having to prove himself to a new manager, and, once again, it wasn't going to be easy. Morell Maison had initially joined the club to oversee the newly formed reserve team and had already told Black that he expected more from him, having accused him of cruising through a reserve match. 'I thought that was a bit much,' says Black, 'but there was a lot more from where that came from. All the lads were saying, "Who is the man?" He just appeared from nowhere, and nobody had a clue who he was.

'We couldn't believe what was happening at the club. There was Imraan in his late twenties hiring and firing managers like there was no tomorrow. He had told us he was going to take his time in appointing the next manager and wasn't going to make a rash decision again.'

Ladak assured Black he would start more games under Maison than he had done under Wilson, but things quickly got on top of him again. Maison signed some players on full-time contracts, who the more experienced players in the squad thought were not good enough for Conference North.

Much to his annoyance, one morning, Black drove all the way to Milton Keynes for training to find the Dons players had been given the day off, but nobody had told him.

Training was moved to a school pitch in Kettering, before being switched to another pitch in the town that was little better. Some of the players who had despaired at Gascoigne's final few weeks were beginning to look back on the previous autumn as the good old days.

Black then refused to turn up for training when he received his wage slip to discover he hadn't been given the promised £100-a-week pay rise as part of the full-time contract. It was rectified, but by then Black felt he would be better off playing part-time again.

Unable to get in the team in his preferred striking role, he put up with playing anywhere from left and right midfield to centre midfield to out on the wing to full-back. But he snapped when, after the final game of the season, he was told he would have to report back for a week of additional training. There was an outstanding reserve game and Maison wanted the entire squad there.

He was also ordered to be at the club's presentation evening a fortnight later, despite having booked an end-of-season holiday before anything about this had been mentioned. For Black, that was the final straw. 'I didn't feel I could play another season under him. He was a likeable person, but he did my head in at times. He'd probably say the same about me.'

Black spoke to Ladak, but the chairman insisted he wasn't going to pay up a contract which had two years to run. Bitterly frustrated, Black thrashed out a deal whereby all but two months of his contract were to be cancelled, although he wouldn't even get that if he went back to Lancaster City.

Having spoken to Phil Wilson at Barrow, Black thought he had a future there. But, following more aggravation for the young player, he returned to Lancaster to sign for his former club, although he asked them not to make it official until he'd had his money off Kettering, which was due in two payments. 'I had received my first payment off Kettering more than a week late and that was after ringing them up at least 10 times,' he claims. 'My last payment was due and I was trying to ring Imraan but he wouldn't answer his phone. I had told everyone at Lancaster to keep it quiet but somehow Imraan must have found out. Then two weeks after I was supposed to get the payment there was a photo shoot in the local paper to model the new kit. It was during the day and nobody else could do it, so I ended up doing it. After that, there was no way of getting that £1,600.'

Within a month of signing for Lancaster, it seemed Black was again being mucked around. The weekly wages that had been paid in full every Saturday started being handed over in dribs and drabs over Saturdays, Tuesdays and Thursdays, then he was paid by a cheque which bounced.

So he was soon on the move again, finally making his way to Barrow before trying and failing to get a deal in Spain. He ended up back at Lancaster City for a third spell, and then set off for Australia, playing for Morwell Pegasus in Victoria. Again it wasn't easy, with a two-month delay over international clearance and registration causing him moments of anxiety.

17

'I'LL GET YOU ROBBIE WILLIAMS'

WHEN Paul Gascoigne was appointed manager of Kettering Town, the players couldn't stop themselves speculating about how they could benefit from having such a high-profile manager. None more so than Wayne Diuk.

In the summer of 2005, the right-back had been promised a testimonial match. He was hoping for an end-of-season kickabout attracting a few hundred paying fans that would, hopefully, raise him three or four thousand pounds. When Gascoigne came on the scene, the stakes soared.

With Peter Mallinger no longer chairman and Kevin Wilson gone, Diuk fretted over whether the club would honour the promises made to him. One evening, during a training session early into the new regime, Diuk approached Gascoigne, and said, 'I don't know if you know, gaffer, but it's my testimonial year.'

Gascoigne held his hands up to silence him. 'He said to me, "Don't you worry, Diuky, I'll sort it for you. I'll fill this ground."'

Gascoigne began reeling off a list of the names he would get to come along. They included Ally McCoist, Ian Wright and Chris Waddle. 'And I'll get you Robbie Williams,' he told the stunned player. 'He said to me, "I can get you 40 grand," and I was like, wow, all I could see was pound signs.'

Gascoigne called Andy Billingham on to the pitch. 'He told me to leave it with Andy and he'd sort it out. After training, I went back into the changing room and all the lads were there. I told them what the gaffer had said and the whole room started laughing at me. Of course, I ended up with none of that. Now whenever I see one of the lads they put on a Geordie accent and say, "I'll get you Robbie Williams."'

'He thought he was going to have Robbie Williams and Hollywood coming to play for him,' laughs Christian Moore. 'He ended up with a race night.'

By the end of the season, and with Gascoigne a memory, Diuk was even refused permission to have his match at Rockingham Road: 'The lads were saying to me, "40 grand – you ain't going to get 40 quid."'

The club's former directors organised a race night and auction for him, but, even then, they had to threaten to take the event elsewhere when they were told they'd have to pay to hire the social club. 'I was very grateful to them for doing it,' says Diuk. 'But I should have had a game. I was there seven years, I played 300 games and I was promised a testimonial. A lot of the Kettering supporters were upset about it.'

In a season of broken promises, Diuk's testimonial was just another. Yet Moore believes that, had Gascoigne stayed at Rockingham Road, he would have delivered. 'My experience of Paul Gascoigne was I don't think he was a devious bloke, I don't think he'd lie to you. He was a genuinely nice bloke and, if he said he was going to get Robbie Williams, then he would try to get you Robbie Williams. I don't think it was something he'd say for the sake of it. He's the type of guy who, if you went to him and said, "I've got nowhere to stay," he'd put you up.'

If anything, Moore felt that one of Gascoigne's difficulties as a manager was that he didn't have it in him to upset his players. He went out of his way to avoid confrontation and was nervous and edgy when he had to tell them they were dropped. 'Him coming to tell me I wasn't in the team probably broke his heart more than mine. He'd get so upset at having to tell you you felt sorry for him.'

Other players agree. Though they were glad to see the back of Gascoigne the manager, it seems they liked Gascoigne the man. 'My memory of him is he's such a nice guy and he'd do anything for you,' recalls Brett Solkhon.

Before the club had lost its way, there had been some nice touches that had meant a lot. Diuk had been named man of the match in Gascoigne's first game and had been presented with his award by Gascoigne in the sponsors' lounge. A photograph had been taken. Before the next match, Diuk was called into the manager's office. 'He handed me an envelope. I opened it and he'd got the picture blown up and signed it: "To Diuky, well done from the boss, Paul Gazza Gascoigne, xx." I've got it framed on a wall in my house. That's something I will keep forever.'

Neil Midgley felt that Gascoigne probably had little understanding of the impact he'd had on a generation of footballers who had grown up in awe of his unique talent. Midgley was mortified to have sworn at Gascoigne during one game and, as things took a turn for the worse, he was hauled off at half-time in the shocking defeat at Redditch.

'I don't know if they were too sure how we were feeling as individuals,' recalls Midgley. 'But this time I stood up and said, "What's going on? I didn't get any service, why are you taking me off?" He didn't really answer. After the game on the bus I was still thinking about it, so I went down to the front and said, "Gaffer, can I have a word?" I told him I wasn't happy about being taken off. Again, he didn't really want to talk about it and just said, "Don't worry, you'll be OK next time."

'I started the next game and scored the winner. The next day he sent me a text message saying, "Well done, that's what I want from you. Excellent. Gazza xxx." I've got that message saved on one of my old phones.

'Something like that from him made you feel so good about yourself. He could be an infectious character. If after a game he gave you a kiss and a hug it would make you feel on top of the world.'

Stalybridge Celtic boss John Reed chuckles as he recalls the kisses he received before and during his side's 4–1 defeat by Kettering in mid-November. He admits he felt half-cut by the time he went to leave after downing the half-pint of whisky he'd been handed by Gascoigne. 'He said to me come to his office and have a drink, but I had to give that a wide berth. I'd had enough. But I asked him if I could have one of their FA Cup balls and he signed one and gave it to me. Then he gave me a massive squeeze.' Reed returned home with his assistant Mark Atkins. 'Mark said to me, "How come you got three kisses? He didn't kiss me!"'

The club raffled the ball a few weeks later and raised £200 for a local charity. It was another bit of good done in the name of Gascoigne, and Reed recalls, 'He was fantastic that day. From the moment we arrived he was so pally. He didn't know me from Adam, and if he saw me now he probably wouldn't remember who I am, but it was a privilege to meet him.'

Like so many others, Reed had smelled the brandy on Gascoigne's breath each time he had been kissed, and found it sad the way in which everything went wrong so quickly. 'It was a shock. Paul Davis was a lovely, down-to-earth bloke and after the game I told him they'd walk that division.

'On the Thursday before the game, I had told my lads I didn't want any of this Gazzamania stuff, I didn't want anyone queuing up for his autograph. We were going there to get three points. But, once you got there, he took over. You couldn't help but love him, what an amazing man. We lost and I loved that day. When he was off the booze, what an experience it must have been going into work with him. He's a legend.'

*   *   *

Looking back on those 39 days, Ladak admits he regularly thinks about whether he was right to sack his boyhood hero. Despite everything that happened, despite Gascoigne's rage and the 'really, really horrible' public spat, Ladak says he has no regrets about taking Gascoigne to Kettering, only that it all ended so badly.

In an interview with Jon Dunham to reflect on events, Ladak revealed, 'Hindsight is a wonderful thing and I look back now and think I could have made things work for Paul. If I had done that, it probably would have been better for him and the club. He has not been in football since I sacked him and I do feel I let him down in a way. I could have stuck with him longer. It might have worked, it might not have worked. But there isn't a day that goes by when I don't think about that decision.'

During their discussions after Ladak's initial approach in the summer of 2005, Gascoigne had spoken of his preference for a Football League club rather than Kettering. Finances made that impractical. Although Gascoigne's profile had generated huge interest in the club, his departure had wide-ranging implications for all the big plans Ladak had drawn up.

With no corporate facilities and unable to develop the stadium because of problems with the lease, Ladak knew it was going to take something special to sell the club to outsiders. 'He put all his eggs in one basket,' says Dave Dunham. 'Suddenly all the eggs were broken.'

'I really believed it would work,' Ladak told Jon Dunham. 'I knew there was a chance that it wouldn't, but I felt we could make it happen. With all the problems the club had, it would have really helped if things had worked with Paul. It's very hard to generate money with the lack of facilities we have and Paul was vital to moving the club forward from a financial point of view.

'From the moment he left, it probably took away 70 to 75 per cent of our potential revenue stream. From the projections we had, I think our income would have at least quadrupled. But, once he went, it left an anti-climactic feeling with everybody and, in actual fact, our revenue dipped.

'Football is about a lot of things but the reality is money talks. Without Paul it took away a lot of our potential ambition. We are still trying to push ahead by gaining promotion and sorting out the ground. But it's a lot harder without the name of Paul Gascoigne.'

Ladak was only 27 when all this happened. He had been unprepared for the extent of the furore generated by both Gascoigne's appointment and his sacking.

'Paul was being advised by a different party and they told me they would do everything they could to drag my name through the mud and make Paul out to be the victim. They kept telling me that Paul was a national icon and the darling of English football and that I was just a doctor. Which, of course, I wasn't. I was under a lot of pressure and on top of everything I had journalists sleeping on my doorstep, 74 missed calls on my mobile phone and papers contacting me and offering six-figure sums for my side of the story.'

It was the steepest possible learning curve for the novice chairman. 'I don't regret bringing Paul Gascoigne into the club. The one thing I do regret is not giving him more time. It was 60 minutes into the Alfreton game and I sat there thinking, "I have made the wrong decision here."'

By then, of course, Wilson was back in charge determined to play anything but sexy football. Gascoigne was back at Champneys.

Christian Moore and Jamie Paterson both spoke about their disappointment at Gascoigne's management, yet each rejected invitations to dish the dirt from national newspapers. 'It was just a disappointment for me,' recalls Moore. 'You don't get many chances to play for players like that. I got to meet my idol but it wasn't a great time. Everything was so in your face. People say that when you meet celebrities they are never how you imagine them to be. Sometimes, perhaps, it's best not to meet them at all. But he wasn't a bad bloke. He was just a bloke with too many problems who'd been given the wrong job.'

One of the biggest problems Gascoigne has to face on a daily basis is alcoholism, the life-threatening addiction that is forever his volcano waiting to erupt. Although Gascoigne reacted with outrage to Ladak's claim of 37 alcohol-related incidents, Ladak never alleged that Gascoigne had been drunk on each occasion, just that alcohol had been a contributory factor.

Ladak has never produced a definitive list of the 37 allegations, but they included drinking white wine and brandy in the boardroom before games, drinking brandy in the manager's office before and after games, as well as at half-time, being found slumped over his desk drunk in the manager's office, taking a cup of coffee topped up with brandy at pitch-side during matches, giving team talks while under the influence, drinking wine on the coach to away games and falling off the team bus, having emptied a bottle of wine on the way to a match.

There were other 'incidents', such as Gascoigne drinking straight from a bottle of Harvey's Bristol Cream in the chairman's office, drinking cider and white wine in The Beeswing ahead of his first appearance at Rockingham Road, and some staff at the Kettering Park Hotel claim he knocked back bottles of wine and brandy as the pressure mounted.

There were also allegations that he had cut short a television interview to walk away to be sick, while it was widely reported that he had been drunk and sworn at a child when he turned on the Christmas lights in the town centre. He had also been drinking the day he paid a minicab driver to take him from Kettering to Leeds just to get away from it all.

Ladak's complaints weren't that each incident of drinking had involved Gascoigne being roaring drunk. But, like others, he had seen how quickly alcohol would affect him and felt that Gascoigne too often was not in a fit state to make the judgments that are part and parcel of being a football manager. Some of the players had played 'spot the bottle' on the team bus, and this was hardly the sort of thing to convince Ladak that the manager was in control of a divided dressing room.

For much of Gascoigne's time at Kettering, the players had been aware there was an issue with alcohol. Those who hadn't seen for themselves Gascoigne falling off the team bus or drinking from a bottle on the way to games were quickly informed by those who had.

But, to them, Gascoigne drinking was never as big an issue as it was to others around the club. They were more put out by the way they felt badly treated over team selections, the insistence on a brand of football few of them felt comfortable with, the mess over full-time contracts and new signings coming in on twice the money many of them were on.

'He'd tell us stories about how he couldn't get to sleep and how he had to have a few cans of Tennent's Super to get himself off,' claims Solkhon. 'They tried to run things as professionally as they could and we started having pre-match meetings in hotels. But it was when we started doing that that we started noticing his drinking. We'd be getting a bus to an away game and he'd take a bottle of wine for the journey. Then when we got to the hotel he'd go to the bar. It was such a shame.'

The drinking really spiralled out of control following the death of George Best. 'He was drunk before the next game, and you could see the parallels between the two players,' recalls Solkhon. 'He'd just go into the directors' lounge, no matter where we were, and get a drink.'

Moore may have lost respect for Gascoigne because of the way he ran away from confrontation, but he never felt alcohol was a massive factor. 'I smelled the alcohol on his breath, and I heard about the wine on the coach, but even when it was obvious he'd had a drink he wasn't necessarily out of it. It was strange how somebody could claim in only 39 days there were 37 drink-related incidents. What did he mean by incidents? There were occasions when he might have had a drink but definitely wasn't drunk. Was that an incident?

'It was obvious Gascoigne was drinking when he came to the club, so who brought him in? If you're an employer and you employ somebody in that situation then doesn't the buck stop with you? Paul got all the flak but I don't think what happened at Kettering was all Paul's fault. Other people were involved. The Paul Gascoigne era was a circus and a lot of people put all that down to just Paul Gascoigne, but I don't think it was. At that time, everything seemed typical of people being in charge of a football club who shouldn't be.'

Ladak had asked Davis to keep an eye on Gascoigne's drinking, but the players agree there was little he could have done to keep the manager off the booze, and some point the finger elsewhere.

'One of Gascoigne's biggest problems was he wasn't helped by the people around him,' claims Jon Dunham. 'He had all these people around him saying they were his friends. They just wanted to be part of the Paul Gascoigne experience and see if they could make money out of him.'

'These so-called friends of Gazza, when do they ever get hold of him and tell him to stop doing what he's doing?' says Diuk. 'It's just, "Here's some more booze and just keep giving me money." I think deep down he's a nice person but people have taken advantage of him, which is wrong.

'I think Imraan brought him to Kettering to help make money and then ditched him. I don't see how he could say 37 drink-related incidents because I don't think Gazza was at the club 37 times in total. I can imagine it being a few, but I'd like to know where the 37 came from.'

Most at the club agreed that Gascoigne had been unable to cope with the pressure of being a manager. The players also found the pressure of playing for such a big name weighing them down. 'Every team we played upped their game, and the pressure just mounted and mounted,' remembers Midgley. 'The games were a lot harder, the training was a lot different, everything was a lot harder to cope with. There was a complete overhaul of everything – training, tactics, match days, players. We were going to away games, they were having a big crowd get behind them and we were disappointed to come away with a draw.

'You're slipping up results-wise and the management are saying we want you to do this and we want you to do that. Yeah, we're trying to do it but it's all got on top of us individually and as a squad. It was very difficult to play your natural game. Then in training we were being told, play this way and you'll win the game. But we couldn't play their way and we stopped winning games.'

Midgley was another to benefit from Gascoigne's willingness to do what he could to keep his players happy. He plucked up the courage to knock on Gascoigne's door and ask him for a pay rise. Gascoigne was straight on the phone to Ladak and got Midgley the money he had asked for.

Gascoigne also got Chris Waddle, another of Midgley's Spurs heroes, to present him with a man-of-the-match award in the sponsors' lounge after one game. 'It's things like that you try to remember. When he first came in he'd say things that weren't really that funny but the boys would be cracking up just because it was him who had said it.

'Get him in a football environment and he's an infectious character, you'd want to do well for him. But a lot of people were waiting for it to go wrong, and you could see the pressure he was putting on himself. Now I just try to remember the good bits – scoring for him, the dentist's chair, meeting my Spurs heroes. He kissed me on the cheek, patted me on the head and told me what a good player I was. You don't forget that. Whenever I tell somebody I played for Kettering, the first thing they say is, "Isn't that where Paul Gascoigne was manager?"'

Midgley believes the pizzas after training were an example of the way Gascoigne tried to improve their lot. 'It was a nice touch, it was just something he wanted to do for us. He'd be saying things like, "I want you to have these," "I want to get boots for you," "I want to get you a contract," "I want to do things for you."'

Darren Lynch, a tough, no-nonsense striker, had been out of action since the final home game of the previous season, having chipped a bone just above his knee. He also tore medial ligaments and injured his cartilage. Shortly after taking over, Gascoigne arranged for Lynch to have a follow-up operation on his badly damaged knee to speed up his recovery. Lynch says, 'I can't have a bad word to say about him. He was a decent guy and whatever problems he had the players did get on well with him personally.'

It wasn't just those within the club who felt the effect of Gascoigne. His first full week at Rockingham Road coincided with the build-up to the first round proper of the FA Cup. Kettering had made it through the qualifying stages thanks to an excellent 3–0 defeat of Gravesend & Northfleet in Kevin Wilson's last game as manager. Gascoigne was by far the biggest name involved in the competition at that stage, so the trophy was brought to Kettering and Gascoigne and Davis went off on a tour of local schools, with Ladak, Mallinger and a posse of FA officials, reporters, photographers and cameramen in tow.

'The kids loved it and, although they were too young to remember him as a player, they seemed to love him,' recalls Mallinger. 'You'd be waiting to go into the school hall and you'd hear them chanting, "Gazza, Gazza," and they'd be so excited.'

Gascoigne was happy to sit among the boys and girls and chat for as long as they wanted. He was natural and warm, and went outside to watch them play a game of football. He enjoyed himself as much as they did and revealed, 'I just want to give something back to the community if I can.'

It was Gascoigne at his best and Geoff Noakes, the head at Millbrook Primary School in Kettering, told him how much it meant to have him visit. 'The children were absolutely spellbound. This is something they will remember for the rest of their lives.'

Another school he took the trophy to was Brambleside Primary. He told the children that the only other time he had touched it was when he was lying in a hospital bed 14 years earlier. He had been stretchered off the pitch at Wembley with ruptured cruciate knee ligaments 17 minutes into the 1991 FA Cup final after a fearsome knee-high tackle on Nottingham Forest's Gary Charles. He tried to play on and collapsed before being rushed to hospital, where he watched the completion of the match on television in bed. Tottenham won 2–1 and Gascoigne's victorious teammates took the trophy to him in hospital that evening. As he recounted the story for the children, his eyes welled up. 'He's a very nice man,' said 10-year-old Tiarnan Nelis.

In those early days, there was plenty of optimism that Gascoigne would have an invigorating effect on the town, which in turn would boost attendances at the football club. Ladak and Billingham were using such occasions to urge the schoolchildren to tell their parents to take them along to watch the team managed by Gazza the legend, while there was plenty of demand for personal visits from Gascoigne.

One saw him launch an exhibition of classic sporting memorabilia in nearby Wellingborough. Among the items on display were signed photographs of Gascoigne at the 1990 World Cup. 'They are good memories,' he told organisers as he studied the pictures intensely for several minutes. Others looked at the pictures of Gascoigne in his youthful prime and compared them to the man standing before them. It brought home quite how badly the years had ravaged him.

There was no doubt that such activity away from the football club was doing Gascoigne's morale a world of good. He seemed to genuinely appreciate people telling him how much he meant to them, and, whatever their age, everyone had a favourite story.

'He seemed very relaxed in this environment and had he been able to remain sober he would have proved a fantastic asset to the club and the town,' maintains Mallinger. 'The trouble was, once back at the club, he reverted to the brandy and white wine routine and Paul Davis would have the job of taking him home.'

Opposition fans also had their memories of Gascoigne the England genius and would queue for an autograph often in the autumn rain and cold. At Hednesford, where Gascoigne's behaviour on a desperately cold November evening caused concern, the one time his face lit up was when the guy manning the burger stall at Keys Park stripped off his apron to reveal an England replica top and strode up to Gascoigne to announce he wanted to shake the hand of 'the best player I ever saw wear an England shirt.'

Things were already starting to unravel for Gascoigne by that game, his fourth. While the novelty factor guaranteed him attention, at least for an hour or two, whenever Gascoigne took to the road, Kettering's supporters wanted events on the pitch to start matching all the big talk. The celebrity spotters had drifted away and hardcore fans had yet to see any big-name signings.

For those like Jon Dunham, it was hard to shake off the feeling that it was going to end in disappointment. 'I think they thought because it was Gascoigne the national media would be around forever. But this was Kettering Town, a non-League club that wasn't even in the Conference. I think it became obvious pretty quickly to Gascoigne that it was miles away from what he was expecting. If they had taken over a Football League club, it might have been different. But nobody outside of Kettering gave two hoots about them regardless of who the manager was.'

After Gascoigne's departure, Kettering's fans spent the rest of that season being taunted by opposing supporters singing, 'Where's your Gazza gone?'

So were his 39 days of any long-term benefit to Kettering Town? While Ladak struggled to pick up the pieces of the downturn in income, many believe that, ultimately, those troubles with Gascoigne helped him cement his place at the club.

'I watched Imraan on television the day he sacked Gascoigne and I wondered if he'd walk away,' reveals Dave Dunham. 'I don't think it was a brave decision to sack him because that was inevitable, but to go on national television to say the man I had brought in has let me down and I'm sacking him, that took guts. I admired Imraan for doing that. I think he had made a mistake in the first place but it's not easy to admit that in front of millions of TV viewers when you're talking about a legend of English football.'

Dunham feels all the attention heaped on the club at that time had a long-lasting benefit. 'Even though it was brief it was one of those defining moments. I wouldn't knock that at all, and it has raised the profile of the football club.'

Ladak admits that, initially, he had seen Kettering as no more than a vehicle to fulfil his personal ambitions, but says he became 'consumed' by the aspirations of the club's supporters. He has worked tirelessly to keep the club moving forward since those explosive first few months.

As for Gascoigne himself, he says he doesn't regret taking the job at Kettering but his experience there only reinforced his belief that people use his name for the publicity, to get attendances up and to attract interest from sponsors. Once they've had all that, they lose interest.

In an ideal world, Gascoigne would have his pick of clubs and the likes of Kettering would be so far down the list they would never appear on his radar. But just as Gascoigne fears others are exploiting him, so those who run football clubs are reluctant to give Gascoigne a chance to exploit them.

Will he ever get the chance to be a football manager again? There have been many negative stories concerning his drinking and other personal problems since leaving Kettering, and the job offers have hardly flooded in. The day Ladak sacked him, he said he had lost faith in Gascoigne's ability to manage with a clear head. The question any chairman would need to ask himself if he was considering appointing Gascoigne as manager is how confident he could be that Gascoigne, whatever the promises, would not make alcohol an issue.

During one of their chats at training, Gascoigne had told Mike Capps that he'd love to be manager of England. You think that's never going to happen? Probably not, but Diego Maradona landed the top job with Argentina despite decades of outrageous behaviour that makes Gascoigne's indiscretions appear very minor.

They might share a problem with alcohol, but Gazza never got suspended from playing for 15 months because of cocaine abuse, never got sent home in disgrace from a World Cup final after failing a drugs test and never got a suspended jail sentence for shooting at journalists with an air rifle. He also doesn't owe nearly 40 million euros in back taxes to the Italian government.

So, can we say never? If Maradona could put all that behind him to become manager of Argentina, a country which has won the World Cup twice and been finalists twice more, perhaps Gascoigne still has some hope with England, however unlikely. Only time will tell.

18

GASCOIGNE'S HIGH PRICE OF FAME

THE GASCOIGNE story was one of the biggest there had been in Northamptonshire, and it needed time and commitment to cover it. You were never sure which Paul Gascoigne you were going to meet, but whatever his mood you couldn't help but love him. Peter Mallinger says that without the alcohol Gascoigne would have been a terrific asset to the football club and the town of Kettering. I'd say that without the alcohol Gascoigne would be a terrific asset to himself.

He drove many of his players to despair in those 39 days. His influence was disruptive and Wayne Diuk speaks for nearly all when he says, 'It was a relief when Gascoigne got the sack – I just wanted to get back to something approaching normality.'

All the players have different stories to tell of their time with him, but there are two things they have in common: firstly, he was their favourite footballer in his prime and, secondly, as their manager, when sober, he was a likeable, lovable guy who would do anything for them. Even Kevin Wilson, who had more reason than most to be upset by his treatment at Gascoigne's hands, calls him 'a really charming bloke'.

During my time at the *Evening Telegraph*, I would write a regular Saturday column, and below is a piece I wrote a few days after Gascoigne had been sacked. I still get choked up when I read it. Each time I met him I was conscious I was in the presence of one of the greatest English footballing talents of all time, and I had desperately wanted him to make a success of the job and prove his critics wrong.

So much of what he has gone through – before, during and after his time at Kettering – has been self-inflicted. But, as Andy Hall asked, 'How in control is he?' That is a simple question that is very, very difficult to answer.

This is what I wrote on Saturday, 10 December 2005:

There is so much to like and love about Paul Gascoigne. Every time I'd met him over the past six weeks I had wanted to wrap my arms around him and tell him to take good care of himself.

This is a man who is battling demons and who has gone through traumas that most of us haven't confronted in our worst nightmares.

The real personal tragedy of events of this week is that Gascoigne has again been deprived of the one drug it seems he finds impossible to live without – football.

His enthusiasm for Kettering Town was genuine. You could see he really did want to make a success of his opportunity here, and his desire to lead Kettering Town into the Football League for the first time in their 133-year history was clear.

Unfortunately, too many things got in the way, and the talk now should not be of football and winning or losing on a sports field. It should be of those people who care about Gazza, and who can influence him, rallying round to give him the support and help he needs to bounce back from this latest setback. Not as a football manager, but as a human being.

I had the chance to get close to Gazza during his time at Rockingham Road, and I'll tell it as I saw it: he was warm, good-humoured, generous, deeply committed to the cause and coped with incredible demands on his time with admirable patience.

Few sportsmen could whip up the hysteria that accompanies him everywhere, and his willingness to sign autographs and pose for pictures was admirable to observe.

But, by the same token, his emotions are never far from the surface and there are things going on in his personal life that are causing him immeasurable misery.

During his short spell in Kettering, he raised the club's and town's profile in a way that was unimaginable before. He has so much goodness in him, and is such a likeable and lovable bloke, that it breaks your heart when it goes wrong.

All I want for a man I admired more than any as a footballer in the 1990s is for him to find the peace and happiness he craves and deserves. There is a price to be paid for fame and fortune. Believe me, Gazza is paying it. I wish him well.

For a short while after his departure, it was believed that Gascoigne would return to the town for the 'Evening with Paul Gascoigne' event scheduled for 14 December at Wicksteed. Some 340 people had purchased tickets in anticipation of an evening in his company, yet nobody was surprised when he failed to show. Billingham was there and took the microphone to tell the gathering, 'Paul Gascoigne has asked me to say a couple of words on his behalf:

"Unfortunately, I am unable to be here tonight. Have a wonderful evening and raise lots of money. I am gutted I cannot be here."'

And as the curtain came down on Gascoigne's brief dalliance with Kettering, a row broke out between Ladak and Billingham over where the proceeds from that event should go. It seemed a fitting finale.

Both John Dunham and I have our mementos from the Gascoigne era, including signed shirts and programmes. We often talk about those crazy days and it invariably ends in laughter. We talk about the occasion when Gascoigne, during a conversation in the social club, told us that he very much wanted us, the local press, on his side in his quest to develop the club. We asked if there were any more signings in the pipeline and he replied that he would make sure we'd have any news as soon as he did. We drove the five minutes back to the office to be greeted by a statement on the Poppies website announcing the signing of Kevin Dixon. Why hadn't he told us? Was it deliberate? Neither of us believes it was. It was just that by this stage he had lost touch with exactly what was happening around him.

Each time we talk, we agree that those 39 days seemed so much longer. More excitement and incident was packed into them than a non-League club could expect in 39 years.

Like me, Dunham has great sympathy for Gascoigne. But, as he says, nobody can cure his addictions for him.

Andy Hall, a young lad whose only dream was to be a professional footballer, saw Gascoigne's arrival as possibly his opportunity to make that dream come true. When asked what he had learned most from the 39 days under his superstar manager, he replied, 'Not to drink.'

What sort of a legacy is that for a man as adored as Paul Gascoigne once was?

What a crying shame.

KEY DATES

2005

6 September
Imraan Ladak makes contact with Peter Mallinger

14 September
Ladak and Mallinger shake hands on agreement for takeover

22 September
Gascoigne meets Mallinger at ground

24 September
Gascoigne watches first match

1 October
Mallinger issues statement confirming he has received an offer for his shares

4 October

Ladak tells Jon Dunham that building new stadium will be top priority for new owners

6 October

Ladak meets representatives from the Supporters Trust to assure them of good intentions

7 October

Alan Biley quits as assistant manager

8 October

Ladak attends FA Cup third-qualifying-round match at St Albans with Paul Davis. He reveals there will be three management positions, director of football, manager and head coach, but refuses to say who will fill each role

11 October

Ladak reveals Gascoigne is to be manager, Davis head coach and Wilson director of football

17 October

Ladak's and Gascoigne's representatives deny reports in Portugal that he is to join Algarve United

19 October

Ladak denies he made an offer for Port Vale, saying, 'The only club we have made a firm offer for is Kettering.'

22 October

Kettering beat Gravesend & Northfleet 3–0 in FA Cup fourth qualifying round. It is Kevin Wilson's last game as manager

27 October

Press conference to announce Gascoigne as manager

28 October

Gascoigne introduces himself to players in series of telephone calls

29 October

Gascoigne's first game as manager. Kettering beat Droylsden 1–0

31 October

Kevin Wilson leaves

1 November

Gascoigne's first training session

5 November

Kettering lose to Stevenage Borough 3–1 in FA Cup first round. Attendance is 4,548, the highest for 11 years

8 November

Gascoigne falls off team bus at Alfreton, where game is called off before kick-off. Gascoigne rants at officials

10 November

Gascoigne reveals Kettering are competing with Tesco for land to build new stadium

12 November

Best win of Gascoigne's time as manager, 4–1 against Stalybridge Celtic

14 November

Kettering draw 2–2 at lowly Hednesford Town after going 2–0 behind. Gascoigne announces from now on the man of the match will get to drive a Lamborghini for a week

16 November

Gascoigne says he will play in an emergency

17 November

Ryan-Zico Black signs from Lancaster Town. Gascoigne announces plans to take training to three evenings a week and for first reserve match

19 November

Kettering draw 1–1 at bottom club Vauxhall Motors

22 November

Kettering lose 2–1 at lowly Redditch United

24 November

Kevin Dixon and Michael McKenzie sign. Jamie Paterson leaves after fall-out with Gascoigne

25 November

George Best dies

26 November

Kettering beat Gainsborough Trinity 1–0 in FA Trophy. Gascoigne turns on Christmas lights in Kettering town centre. He is accused of being drunk

27 November

On spur of the moment, Gascoigne pays a minicab driver £300 to drive him to Leeds

30 November

Jordan Fowler, a product of the Arsenal youth academy, signs

1 December

Ladak announces plans for full-time players to train with MK Dons

3 December

George Best's funeral. Kettering lose 3–1 at home to Barrow. Ladak and Gascoigne clash, and Ladak sacks Gascoigne

4 December

Gascoigne goes to Birmingham to stay with Billingham. A tearful Gascoigne rings some players to ask, 'Are you with me?'

5 December

Official announcement of Gascoigne's dismissal. Kevin Wilson is new manager. Gascoigne goes to Liverpool and threatens to attend next day's game. Gascoigne arrested after photographer is assaulted

6 December

Gascoigne released from police cell and returns to Champneys. Wilson takes charge for 1–1 draw at Alfreton

8 December

Jamie Paterson returns as player-coach

2006

11 January
Kettering lose to Worcester City and drop into bottom half of Nationwide North table

13 January
Kettering go out of FA Trophy, losing 2–1 to Dagenham & Redbridge

14 January
Anthony Elding signs from Stevenage Borough for a 'package' of £40,000

31 January
Neil Midgley released. Christian Moore moves to Burton Albion, initially on loan

1 February
Kevin Wilson sacked

2 February
Morell Maison appointed manager with Alan Biley assistant manager. Club captain Derek Brown leaves for Nuneaton

3 February
Neil Midgley returns

8 February
Moses Olaleye signs from Buckingham Town

9 February
Wilson appointed manager of Hucknall Town

14 February

Nathan Koo-Boothe signs from MK Dons

12 March

Hugh McAuley and Daniel Thompson leave

1 April

Parys Okai signs from Hitchin Town and Serge Makofo from MK Dons

23 April

Play-off hopes end

1 May

Maison appointed manager on permanent basis following 'successful spell as caretaker manager'

3 May

Anthony Elding and Alan Biley leave

11 May

Striker Rene Howe signs from Bedford Town and defender Mark Burrows from Corby Town

19 May

Wayne Diuk, Ollie Burgess, Ryan-Zico Black, Anthony Elding, Jamie Paterson and Michael McKenzie are released

THE EIGHT GAMES UNDER GASCOIGNE

Player marks as given in the *Evening Telegraph* reports of games.

Saturday, 29 October
Kettering Town 1 Droylsden 0
(Conference North)

Scorer: Moore

Kettering: Osborn 7, Diuk 8, McIlwain 8, Theobald 8, Morley 7 (Moore 49 min 7), Hall 8, McAuley 8, Paterson 7, Gould 7, Midgley 7, Burgess 7. Subs not used: Brown, Difante, Duffy, Attwood. Attendance: 2,060 (away fans: 20)

Saturday, 5 November
Kettering Town 1 Stevenage Borough 3
(FA Cup first round)

Scorer: Midgley

Kettering: Osborn 6, Diuk 7, McIlwain 7, Brown 7, Nicell 5, Hall 7, Theobald 6, Paterson 7, Gould 5, Midgley 8 (Difante 74min), Moore 6 (Burgess 74 min). Subs not used: Thompson, Attwood, Duffy
Attendance: 4,548 (away fans: 1,150)

Saturday, 12 November
Kettering Town 4 Stalybridge Celtic 1
(Conference North)

Scorers: Gould, Theobald, Burgess, Moore

Kettering: Osborn 7, Diuk 7, McIlwain 8, Brown 7, Morley 7, Burgess 8, Hall 8 (McAuley 74 min), Theobald 7, Gould 9, Moore 7, Midgley 7. Subs not used: Thompson, Duffy, Nicell, Paterson
Attendance: 1,478 (away fans: 75)

Monday, 14 November
Hednesford Town 2 Kettering Town 2
(Conference North)

Scorers: Moore, Gould
Kettering: Osborn 6, Diuk 7, McIlwain 6, Brown 6, Morley 6, Burgess 7 (Duffy 57min), Hall 7 (Paterson 76 min), Theobald 7, Gould 7, Moore 7, Midgley 8 (Difante 82 min). Subs not used: Thompson, Nicell
Attendance: 992 (away fans: 160)

Saturday, 19 November
Vauxhall Motors 1 Kettering Town 1
(Conference North)

Scorer: Duffy
Kettering: Osborn 7, Diuk 7, McIlwain 7, Brown 6 (Paterson 26min 6), Morley 7, Burgess 6, Theobald 7, Hall 6, Gould 6, Duffy 7 (Black 54min), Moore 6 (Difante 66 min). Subs not used: Midgley, Nicell
Attendance: 383 (away fans: 130)

Tuesday, 22 November
Redditch United 2 Kettering Town 1
(Conference North)

Scorer: Gould
Kettering: Osborn 5, Nicell 6, McIlwain 5, Diuk 5, Morley 4, Burgess 4 (Black 45 min 5), Theobald 5, Hall 6, Gould 5, Midgley 5 (Paterson 45 min 5), Moore 5. Subs not used: Thompson, Attwood, Difante
Attendance: 753 (away fans: 150)

Saturday, 26 November
Kettering Town 1 Gainsborough Trinity 0

Scorer: Midgley

Kettering: Osborn 6, Nicell 6, Diuk 6, McIlwain 7, Morley 5, Hall 6, Gould 6 (Dixon 86 min), Theobald 5, Burgess 6, Duffy 7 (McKenzie 71 min), Midgley 7. Subs not used: Difante, Thompson, Black

Attendance: 1,132 (away fans: 10)

Saturday, 3 December
Kettering Town 1 Barrow 3
(Conference North)

Scorer: Moore

Kettering: Osborn 6, Diuk 5, McIlwain 6, Brown 5, Morley 6, Hall 6 (Fowler 58 min 5), Theobald 5, Gould 5, Burgess 7, Midgley 5 (Moore 15 min 6), Duffy 5 (McKenzie 45 min 6). Subs not used: Nicell, Dixon

Attendance: 1,272 (away fans: 30)

HOW THE LINE-UPS CHANGED
Only five of the players who started Paul's Gascoigne's last game in charge on 3 December were in the team that played the final game of that season under Morell Maison. Here are the teams sent out by Kevin Wilson for the last games of his first and second spells as manager, Gascoigne's last game and the last game of the season under Maison.

22 October
Kettering Town 3 Gravesend & Northfleet 0
(manager: Kevin Wilson)

Mark Osborn, Wayne Diuk, Craig McIlwain, David Theobald, Stephan Morley, Andy Hall, Liam Nicell, Jamie

Paterson, James Gould, Neil Midgley, Robert Duffy. Subs: Derek Brown, Chris Difante, Daniel Thompson, Craig Attwood, Mark Njotsa

3 December
Kettering 1 Barrow 3
(manager: Paul Gascoigne)
Mark Osborn, Wayne Diuk, Craig McIlwain, Derek Brown, Stephan Morley, Andy Hall, David Theobald, James Gould, Ollie Burgess, Neil Midgley, Robert Duffy. Subs: Liam Nicell, Christian Moore, Michael McKenzie, Jordan Fowler, Kevin Dixon

29 January
Hyde United 3 Kettering Town 0
(manager: Kevin Wilson)
Mark Osborn, Wayne Diuk, Derek Brown, Craig McIlwain, James Gould, Ollie Burgess, Hugh McAuley, Jamie Paterson, Dean Brennan, Jermaine Palmer, Anthony Elding. Subs: Christian Moore, Ryan-Zico Black, Andy Hall, David Theobald, Ryan Young

29 April
Kettering 2 Workington 1
(manager: Morell Maison)
Mark Osborn, Nathan Koo-Boothe, Craig McIlwain, David Theobald, Andy Hall, Brett Solkhon, Stephan Morley, Ollie Burgess, Parys Okai, Patrick Peter, Junior McDougald. Subs: Liam Nicell, Darren Lynch, Moses Olaleye, Serge Makofo, Ryan-Zico Black